ESSENTIAL ADMINISTRATIVE LAW

Third Edition

Cavendish
Publishing
Pty Limited

Sydney • London • Portland, Oregon

Titles in the series:

ESSENTIAL ADMINISTRATIVE LAW

Third Edition

Ian Ellis-Jones, BA, LLB, LLM, DD,
Grad Dip Leg Prac, Adv Mang Cert,
Senior Lecturer, Faculty of Law,
University of Technology, Sydney

General Editor
Professor David Barker
Dean of the Faculty of Law,
University of Technology, Sydney

Cavendish
Publishing
Pty Limited

Sydney • London • Portland, Oregon

Third edition first published in Great Britain 2003 by
Cavendish Publishing Limited, The Glass House,
Wharton Street, London WC1X 9PX, United Kingdom
Telephone: + 44 (0)20 7278 8000   Facsimile: + 44 (0)20 7278 8080
Email: info@cavendishpublishing.com
Website: www.cavendishpublishing.com

Published in the United States by Cavendish Publishing
c/o International Specialized Book Services,
5804 NE Hassalo Street, Portland,
Oregon 97213-3644, USA

Published in Australia by Cavendish Publishing (Australia) Pty Ltd
45 Beach Street, Coogee, NSW 2034, Australia
Telephone: + 61 (2)9664 0909   Facsimile: + 61 (2)9664 5420
Email: info@cavendishpublishing.com.au
Website: www.cavendishpublishing.com.au

© Ellis-Jones, I	2003
First edition	1997
Second edition	2001
Third edition	2003
Reprinted	2007

National Library of Australia Cataloguing in Publication Data
Data available

Library of Congress Cataloguing in Publication Data
Data available

ISBN 10: 1-87690-519-0
ISBN 13: 978-1-87690-519-4

Printed and bound in Great Britain

Foreword

This book is part of the Cavendish Essential Series. The books in the series constitute a unique publishing venture for Australia in that they are intended as a helpful revision aid for the hard-pressed student. They are not intended to be a substitute for the more detailed textbooks which are already listed in the current Cavendish catalogue.

Each book follows a prescribed format consisting of a checklist covering each of the areas in the chapter, and an expanded treatment of 'Essential' issues looking at examination topics in depth.

The authors are all Australian law academics who bring to their subjects a wealth of experience in academic and legal practice.

Professor David Barker
General Editor
Dean of the Faculty of Law,
University of Technology, Sydney

Preface

It is utopian, indeed *Wednesbury* unreasonable (see *Associated Provincial Picture Houses Ltd v Wednesbury Corporation* [1948] 1 KB 223, pp 230 and 234, *per* Lord Greene MR), to suppose that the passing – and not necessarily mere passing – of an examination is not a major aim of students studying administrative law (or, for that matter, any other subject), and idle to pretend that they will not use, or do not need, a revision aid to help them do it.

The primary purpose of this book is to provide such an aid for the undergraduate administrative law student. The book, which is also designed for legal practitioners and administrators who wish to confirm or update prior knowledge, is intended to complement, but not serve as a substitute for, existing textbooks and casebooks on the subject.

The book covers the major topics associated with the subject. Where appropriate, brief case examples are presented to illustrate important principles. In each section, the reader is provided with a revision checklist and guidance on the study of essential issues that figure prominently in examinations.

The law is stated as at 1 September 2003.

Ian Ellis-Jones
September 2003

Acknowledgments

I acknowledge the support and love of my wife Elspeth. Thanks are also due to Rajiv Viswanathan, Solicitor, for his research, editorial assistance, comments and advice. I acknowledge my debt to my former lecturers in law and others who have inspired me over the years, in particular the late Professor John Anderson of the University of Sydney. My appreciation also extends to all my students, past and present, who put up with me during the preparation of the book, and otherwise.

Finally, this book is dedicated to my late parents, Harry and Phyl, who believed in me and taught me to be honest and always to strive for the best.

Contents

Table of Cases

R v Gaming Board for Great Britain
    ex p Benaim and Khaida [1970] 2 QB 417 42

R v Glenelg Town ex p Pier House Pty Ltd (1968) 69

R v Greater Manchester Coroner ex p Tal [1984] 3 WLR 643 88

R v Guardians of Lewisham Union [1897] 1 QB 498 104

R v Hendon RDC ex p Chorley [1933] 2 QB 696 101

R v Hickman ex p Fox and Clinton (1945) 70 CLR 598 . . . . .82, 98

R v Home Office ex p Brind [1991] 1 AC 696 . . . . .8, 66

R v Hull University Visitor ex p Page (1992) 3 WLR 1112 88

R v ILEA ex p Westminster Council [1986] 1 All ER 19 . . . . .63, 64

R v Industrial Commission of South Australia
    ex p Adelaide Milk Supply Co-operative Ltd
    (No 2) (SA Sup Ct, 1978) 89

R v Intervention Board for Agricultural Produce
    ex p ED & F Man (Sugar) Ltd [1986] 2 All ER 115 .19

R v Kirby ex p Boilermakers' Society of Australia (1956) 94 CLR 254 4

R v Knightsbridge Crown Court ex p International
    Sporting Club (London) Ltd [1982] 1 QB 304 85

R v Liverpool Corp ex p Liverpool Taxi Fleet
    Operators' Association [1972] 2 QB 299 . . . . .34, 102

R v MacKellar ex p Ratu (1977) 137 CLR 461 31

R v Medical Appeal Tribunal ex p Gilmore [1957] 1 QB 574 96

R v Morton [1892] 1 QB 39 105

R v Murray and Cormie ex p Commonwealth
    (1916) 22 CLR 437 95

R v North ex p Oakey [1927] 1 KB 491 42

R v Northumberland Compensation Appeal Tribunal
    ex p Shaw [1952] 1 KB 338 . . . . .8, 85

R v Port of London Authority
    ex p Kynoch Ltd [1919] 1 KB 176 69

R v Rand (1866) LR 1 QB 230 45

R v Secretary of State for the Environment ex p Ostler
    [1977] QB 122 97

R v Stafford JJ ex p Stafford Corporation (1940) 102

R v Stepney Corp [1902] 1 KB 317 . . . . .70, 71

R v Surrey JJ (1870) LR 5 QB 466 101

R v Sussex JJ ex p McCarthy [1924] 1 KB 256 45–47

R v Thames Magistrates ex p Polemis [1974] 1 WLR 1371 43

R v Toohey (Aboriginal Land Commissioner)
    ex p Northern Land Council (1981) 56 ALJR 164 . . . . .9, 17, 60

R v Torquay Licensing JJ ex p Brockman [1951] 2 KB 784 70

1 Introduction

You should be familiar with the following areas:

- the scope, nature and content of administrative law
- the development of administrative law
- the nature and role of judicial review
- 'red light' and 'green light' approaches to administrative law and theories of judicial review

The scope, nature and content of administrative law

> Public bodies and Ministers must be compelled to observe the law; and it is essential that bureaucracy should be kept in its place.
>
> *Bradbury v Enfield London Borough Council* (1967),
> *per* Danckwerts LJ

Administrative law is:

- a branch of 'public law';
- primarily concerned with the functions, powers and obligations of:
  - ⊃ the executive arm of government (including the administration); and
  - ⊃ certain non-governmental bodies (known as 'domestic tribunals').

The main focus is on 'judicial review', that is, the exercise of the inherent supervisory jurisdiction of superior courts in relation to decisions made by inferior courts, statutory tribunals, administrative authorities and domestic tribunals.

However, administrative law is also concerned with:

- extra-judicial 'administrative review' of decisions made by administrators; and
- other mechanisms designed to secure the accountability of decision makers.

The meaning of the word 'administrative'

The word 'administrative' is:

- incapable of precise definition; and
- capable of bearing a wide range of meanings.

In phrases such as 'administrative law' and 'administrative tribunal', the word 'administrative' refers to a broad range of governmental (and even, in the case of so called 'domestic tribunals', non-governmental) activity of a non-legislative and non-judicial nature.

For the most part, the courts:

- have considered it inappropriate to seek to expound definitively the meaning and ambit of the expression 'administrative'; and
- have generally taken the approach that what is 'administrative' in nature or character should be determined progressively in each case as particular questions arise.

However, what is 'administrative' will include, for example, the application of a general policy or rule to particular cases (see *Hamblin v Duffy* (1981)), and even ministerial acts are often described as 'administrative'.

Contrary to the view expressed in the *Report of the Committee on Ministers' Powers* (1932), an 'administrative' decision maker:

- may need to consider and weigh submissions and arguments and collate evidence (in addition to acting on the basis of evidence); and
- does not have an unfettered discretion as to the grounds upon which to act nor the means which the decision maker takes to inform itself before acting.

Furthermore, even a large number of so called 'administrative' decisions may and do involve, in greater or less degree, certain of the attributes of a so called 'judicial' or 'quasi-judicial' decision. The oft-cited 'duty to act judicially', in the context of administrative decision making, now refers to a duty to act 'fairly' in the sense of according procedural fairness in the making of any administrative decision that affects a person's rights, interests or legitimate expectations: see *Kioa v West* (1985).

Development of administrative law

The development of a, by no means coherent, set of principles which we now label 'administrative law' is a relatively recent aspect of the common law.

In 1885, the English constitutional lawyer AV Dicey stated in his *Introduction to the Study of the Law of the Constitution*:

> The words 'administrative law' ... are unknown to the English judges and counsel, and are in themselves hardly intelligible without further explanation.

Indeed, Dicey viewed administrative discretion as arbitrary power which ought to be controlled by the courts.

Dicey's rather extreme view of the supremacy of Parliament left administrative law:

- with a great mistrust of executive action; but
- without any theoretical basis for its control; and
- largely neglected until fairly recent times.

In the landmark House of Lords decision in *Ridge v Baldwin* (1964), Lord Reid said:

> We do not have a developed system of administrative law perhaps because until fairly recently we did not need it.

In recent years, there has been a shift of real power from the legislature to the executive (whose various tasks are increasingly undertaken by government departments and other authorities), largely due to the:

- emergence of the 'cabinet system' of government;
- erosion of the doctrine of ministerial responsibility; and
- conferment of broad discretionary powers upon members of the executive and public servants.

The growth of executive power generated a need for an increase in the scope of judicial review of executive and administrative action. To quote Lord Denning MR in *Moorgate Ltd v Twitchings* (1975), 'as Parliament has done nothing, it is time the courts did something'.

Indeed, the real tenor of administrative law is the extent to which the courts and other special tribunals are prepared to scrutinise, and pass judgment on, the actions of administrators.

The so called 'ebb and flow' of administrative law – periods of judicial activism followed by periods of judicial restraint – is to a large extent explained by the fact that, in Australia, there is no strict separation of powers (with the exception of the separation of judicial and executive powers at the federal level): see *R v Kirby ex p Boilermakers' Society of Australia* (1956).

As a result, there is the ability for one organ of government to control, or at least interfere with, the exercise of the functions of another organ of government and even to exercise those functions.

Although this is at times disturbing (for example, when the legislature exercises judicial power and makes a so called 'legislative judgment'), there is, at best, a healthy and dynamic tension between the three organs of government.

The interplay between the various organs of government is the arena in which administrative law is grounded and has its being.

This is well illustrated when one considers the subject of subordinate or delegated legislation:

- The legislature delegates its law making power to the executive.
- The executive exercises that power and makes statutory rules having the force of law.
- Such rules may be disallowed by the legislature or declared invalid by the courts.

Judicial review

In *Church of Scientology v Woodward* (1982), Brennan J described judicial review in the following terms:

> Judicial review is neither more nor less than the enforcement of the rule of law over executive action; it is the means by which executive action is prevented from exceeding the powers and functions assigned to the executive by law and the interests of the individual are protected accordingly.

However, as Frankfurter J pointed out in *Trop v Dulles* (1958):

> ... Judicial power ... must be on guard against encroaching upon its proper bounds, and not the less so since the only restraint upon it is self-restraint.

In judicial review proceedings, the superior court:

- has a supervisory role to ensure compliance with the law; but
- may not, in the absence of express statutory authority, review the administrative decision 'on its merits'.

As Mason J (as he then was) pointed out in *Minister for Aboriginal Affairs v Peko-Wallsend Ltd* (1986):

> It is not the function of the court to substitute its own decision for that of the administrator by exercising a discretion which the legislature has vested in the administrator. Its role is to set limits on the exercise of the discretion, and a decision made within those boundaries cannot be impugned ...

Case example

> A commissioner of inquiry had recommended that certain land be granted to Aboriginal claimants pursuant to certain Commonwealth Aboriginal land rights legislation. The subject land included a uranium deposit over which the respondents had applied for mineral leases. The companies, unhappy with the commissioner's report, made numerous submissions to successive ministers. The responsible minister of the day nevertheless decided to adopt the commissioner's recommendation on the basis of a departmental brief which did not refer to the respondents' submissions. The High Court of Australia held that the minister was bound, as a matter of law, to consider submissions put to the minister by parties who may be adversely affected by the decision and who sought to correct, contradict, elucidate or update material in the commissioner's report. The minister was found not to have taken into account a 'relevant consideration' which the minister was bound, as opposed to entitled, to take into consideration. The court additionally stated that its conclusion and reasoning also conformed to the 'principles of natural justice' (even though it had not been argued in the case that the failure to consider the respondents' submissions amounted to a denial of natural justice).

Minister for Aboriginal Affairs v Peko-Wallsend Ltd (1986)

John McMillan ('Developments under the ADJR Act: the grounds of review' (1991) 20 FLR 50) has correctly pointed out that:

> It has long been a feature of administrative law that ambiguous standards and contrasting principles provide the margin between restraint and intervention, validity and invalidity.

Thus, the superior courts, in the exercise of their inherent supervisory jurisdiction over inferior courts, statutory tribunals, domestic tribunals, and administrative decision makers generally, have developed numerous contrasting distinctions and dichotomies, such as the following:

MERITS .... LAWFULNESS

JUSTICIABLE .... NON-JUSTICIABLE

ADMINISTRATIVE .... JUDICIAL

ADMINISTRATIVE .... LEGISLATIVE

ADMINISTRATIVE .... POLICY

REGULATE .... PROHIBIT

FAIR .... UNFAIR

MANDATORY .... DIRECTORY

RELEVANT .... IRRELEVANT

PROPER .... IMPROPER

REASONABLE .... UNREASONABLE

PROPORTIONATE .... DISPROPORTIONATE

FACT .... LAW

JURISDICTIONAL .... NON-JURISDICTIONAL

FLEXIBLE .... INFLEXIBLE

CERTAIN .... UNCERTAIN

CONSISTENT .... INCONSISTENT

The world is not to be divided into sheep and goats. Not all things are black nor all things white. ... Only the human mind invents categories and tries to force facts into separated pigeon-holes.

Alfred C Kinsey, *Sexual Behavior in the Human Male*, 1948

Grounds of judicial review of administrative action

The following is adapted from Lord Diplock's classification in *Council of Civil Service Unions v Minister for the Civil Service* (1985).

1 Unfairness

- No hearing
- Bias
- No evidence
- No reasons/inquiries

2 Illegality

- *Ultra vires*
  - ⊃ Lack of power
  - ⊃ Abuse of power
  - ⊃ Failure to exercise power
- Jurisdictional error
  - ⊃ Lack of jurisdiction
  - ⊃ Excess of jurisdiction
  - ⊃ Failure to exercise jurisdiction

3 Irrationality

- Manifest unreasonableness (cf abuse of power)
- No rational basis for decision (cf no evidence)
- Arbitrary conduct, perversity

4 Lack of proportionality

- cf irrationality (in particular, manifest unreasonableness)

Grounds of judicial review

There are various ways of classifying the grounds of judicial review.

One method of classification makes the doctrine of *ultra vires* the basis of judicial review, whether there has been a breach of the rules of procedural fairness, lack of power, lack or excess of jurisdiction, non-compliance with statutory procedural requirements, or 'manifest unreasonableness': see *Associated Provincial Picture Houses Ltd v Wednesbury Corporation* (1948). See Oliver, D, 'Is the *ultra vires* rule the basis of judicial review?' [1987] Pub L 543.

The only exception was the *intra vires* ground for review known as 'error of law on the face of the record': see *R v Northumberland Compensation Appeal Tribunal ex p Shaw* (1952).

In *Council of Civil Service Unions v Minister for the Civil Service* (1985), Lord Diplock classified the various grounds of review under the following three heads:

1 'Illegality' – embracing errors traditionally subsumed within the doctrines of *ultra vires* (other than procedural *ultra vires*) and jurisdictional error (as well as error of law on the face of the record).

2 'Irrationality' – that is, manifest (*Wednesbury*) unreasonableness.

3 'Procedural impropriety' – rather than failure to observe the rules of procedural fairness – including procedural *ultra vires*.

In recent years, some jurists (for example, Kirby J) and academics have suggested that there is a fourth ground of review – lack of proportionality: see *State of New South Wales v Macquarie Bank Ltd* (1992); cf *R v Home Office ex p Brind* (1991).

Although Lord Diplock's method of classification has received general acceptance in England, Australian courts, for the most part, continue to classify the grounds of review in fairly traditional terms, *viz*, procedural fairness (natural justice), *ultra vires*, and jurisdictional error (including error of law on the face of the record). One reason is that most Australian courts – unlike their British counterparts – continue to make a distinction between the two otherwise conceptually indistinguishable doctrines of *ultra vires* and jurisdictional error, with the latter, for historical and jurisprudential reasons, being more commonly invoked in the context of inferior courts and quasi-judicial statutory tribunals.

Justiciability

The cornerstone of judicial review is the concept of 'justiciability'.

A 'justiciable' decision is one fit for judicial review; a 'non-justiciable' one is not. However, in recent years the threshold of judicial review has moved considerably, such that many matters which were once considered to be 'non-justiciable' are now 'justiciable', or at least potentially so.

In *ex p R (ex rel Warringah Shire Council); Re Barnett* (1967), the NSW Court of Appeal held that a decision of the NSW Governor-in-Council to dismiss a local council was not reviewable on the ground of denial of procedural fairness. However, decisions made by the Crown's representatives have since been held to be reviewable in appropriate cases on the standard grounds of review: see, for example, *Banks v Transport Regulation Board (Vic)* (1968); *Treasury Gate Pty Ltd v Rice* (1972); *R v Toohey (Aboriginal Land Commissioner) ex p Northern Land Council* (1981); *FAI Insurances Ltd v Winneke* (1981). See also *De Verteuil v Knaggs* (1918).

In other cases, it has been held, or at least strongly suggested, that the standard grounds of review could be applied to such decisions as the decision of a security intelligence organisation (see *Church of Scientology Inc v Woodward* (1982) and *Alister v R* (1984); cf *Council of Civil Service Unions v Minister for the Civil Service* (1985)), to an exercise of legislative power (see *Bread Manufacturers of NSW v Evans* (1981)), and perhaps even to a decision of Cabinet itself (see the discussion in *Minister for Arts, Heritage and Environment v Peko-Wallsend Ltd* (1987), and *South Australia v O'Shea* (1987)).

The fundamental question would now appear to be whether, having regard to its nature and subject matter, the decision *should* be subject to judicial review. Thus, the primary emphasis is now placed on the decision, as opposed to the decision maker.

'Red light' and 'green light' approaches

There are so called 'red light' and 'green light' approaches to administrative law and theories of judicial review:

* The 'red light' theorist generally advocates a more interventionist approach by the courts to the review of administrative decisions.

- The 'green light' theorist, while also acknowledging the need for and importance of judicial review and the rule of law, tends to place more emphasis on non-judicial remedies and procedures (for example, political processes, internal and external administrative review, consultative decision making, etc).

2 Subordinate Legislation

You should be familiar with the following areas:

- the statutory requirements with respect to the making, publication and commencement of statutory rules
- parliamentary review of statutory rules
- judicial review of statutory rules
- the grounds for invalidity of statutory rules

Introduction

'Subordinate legislation' comprises those legislative instruments made by persons or bodies (other than the legislature) to whom or to which the power to legislate has been delegated by the legislature.

Legislation cannot be made by a person or body other than the legislature without the express authority of the legislature. The authority is given by means of an Act of Parliament.

Subordinate legislation:

- is 'subordinate' to the 'primary' legislation, being the statute pursuant to which it is made;
- is also referred to as 'delegated legislation' by reason of the fact that the law making power has been delegated; and
- may take various forms (for example, rules, regulations, by-laws, ordinances).

Making, publication and commencement of statutory rules

In each jurisdiction, there exist special statutory requirements with respect to the making, publication and commencement of statutory rules.

For example, s 39(1) of the Interpretation Act 1987 (NSW) requires that a statutory rule (for example, a regulation) must be published in the Government *Gazette* and provides that the rule takes effect:

- on the day on which it is published; or
- if a later day is specified in the rule for that purpose, on the later day so specified.

Thus, a statutory rule, at least in NSW, cannot be retrospective in its operation; cf s 48(2) of the Acts Interpretation Act 1901 (Cth), which permits federal regulations to have a non-prejudicial retrospective effect .

A statutory rule may specify different days for the commencement of different portions of the rule: see, for example, s 39(2) of the Interpretation Act 1987 (NSW).

In some jurisdictions, there are other important requirements regarding the making of statutory rules.

For example, the Subordinate Legislation Act 1989 (NSW) contains statutory guidelines as to the making of such rules, and imposes requirements with respect to:

- the preparation of 'regulatory impact statements';
- consultation with affected persons; and
- the publication of information relating to proposed statutory rules.

The Act also:

- repealed (with limited exceptions) all NSW statutory rules made before 1 September 1990 in five stages ending on 1 September 1995; and
- provides that any statutory rule made on or after 1 September 1990 is to be repealed five years after it is made.

See s 48 of the Acts Interpretation Act 1901 (Cth), and the Statutory Rules Publication Act 1903 (Cth), as regards the notification (cf publication) and printing of federal statutory rules.

Parliamentary review of statutory rules

In each jurisdiction, there also exist special statutory requirements with respect to parliamentary review of statutory rules.

For example, s 40(1) of the Interpretation Act 1987 (NSW) makes provision for the tabling of statutory rules. However, failure to lay a written notice before each House of Parliament does not affect the validity of a rule: see s 40(4).

Either House of Parliament may then pass a resolution disallowing a statutory rule. On the passing of such a resolution, the rule ceases to have effect: see s 41(2).

Judicial review of subordinate legislation

A piece of subordinate legislation may be ruled invalid by a superior court.

As Holt CJ pointed out in *City of London v Wood* (1702):

> ... every by-law is a law, and as obligatory to all persons bound by it ... as any Act of Parliament, only with this difference, that a by-law is liable to have its validity brought into question.

In the House of Lords' decision in *McEldowney v Forde* (1971), Lord Diplock enunciated a threefold task to determine whether a piece of subordinate legislation is valid:

> ... first to determine the meaning of the words used in the Act of Parliament itself to describe the subordinate legislation which that authority is authorised to make, secondly to determine the meaning of the subordinate legislation itself and finally to decide whether the subordinate legislation complies with that description.

A sample general regulation making power is as follows:

> The Governor may make regulations, not inconsistent with this Act, for or with respect to any matter that by this Act is required or permitted to be prescribed or that is necessary or convenient to be prescribed for carrying out or giving effect to this Act and, in particular, for or with respect to:
> (a) ...
> (b) ...
> (c) ...

A statutory rule will be 'inconsistent' with the statute under which it was purportedly made if it runs counter to the object, purpose, terms or effect of the statute: see *Moreton v The Union Steamship Company of New Zealand Ltd* (1951).

A 'necessary or convenient' power is wider than a 'necessary' power: see *Gibson v Mitchell* (1928).

The word 'necessary':

- does not, in this context, mean 'absolutely essential': see *Commonwealth v Progress Advertising & Press Agency Co Pty Ltd* (1910); but
- generally refers to something that is 'reasonably required' or 'legally ancillary' to the accomplishment of a thing: see *Attorney General v Walker* (1849).

In any event, the words 'necessary or convenient' are strictly ancillary and will not authorise the making of a statutory rule which purports to:

- widen the objects or purposes of the enabling statute; or
- otherwise alter or depart from the statutory scheme or the legislative intention.

Invalidity of subordinate legislation

1 Non-compliance with formal requirements.

2 No enabling power outside the prescribed limits of that power or unconstitutionality.

3 Inconsistency with, or repugnancy to, primary legislation or general law.

4 Improper purpose.

5 Unreasonableness.

6 Lack of proportionality.

7 Uncertainty.

8 Sub-delegation.

The words 'carrying out or giving effect to [the] Act' – and there would appear to be little, if any, difference between those two expressions – standing on their own, confer the same power as the words 'necessary or convenient': see *Clements v Bull* (1953).

Where, as is often the case, a general regulation making power is supplemented by a number of specific heads of regulation making power (whether or not using the words 'without limiting the generality of the foregoing provisions'), a reviewing court:

- will interpret the specific powers in such a way that they do not exceed the general power; but
- will not read down the general regulation making power by reason only of the enumeration of the specific heads of power: see *ex p Provera; Re Wilkinson* (1952).

Grounds for invalidity of statutory rules

A statutory rule may be declared invalid on any one or more of a number of *ultra vires* grounds. (See also Chapter 4.)

Non-compliance with formal requirements

A statutory rule may be declared invalid if the formal requirements that have to be complied with when making the instrument (for example, publication in the *Gazette*) have not been followed: see *O'Keefe v City of Caulfield* (1945).

Simple excess of power

A statutory rule may be declared invalid if it:

- purports to deal with some matter outside the scope of the enabling power; or
- deals with a matter ostensibly within the scope of the enabling power but exceeds the prescribed limits of the power: see *Carbines v Powell* (1925); *Shanahan v Scott* (1956).

Case example

> A regulation, made under the Wireless Telegraphy Act 1905 (Cth), purported to prohibit the manufacture of equipment for use as broadcast receivers. The Act related to the establishment and

operation of wireless telegraphy stations. The High Court, having found that the statute made no provision relating to the manufacture of such equipment, struck down the regulation for going beyond the field marked out by the Act.

Carbines v Powell (1925)

The true nature and purpose of the power must be determined; a connection between the subject of the power and that of the rule is not necessarily sufficient: see *Williams v Melbourne Corporation* (1933).

Inconsistency or repugnancy

A statutory rule may be declared invalid on the ground that it is:

- inconsistent with; or
- repugnant to,

the statute under which it is made, another statute or the general law. See, generally, *Moreton v The Union Steamship Company of New Zealand Ltd* (1951).

A statutory rule creating (and authorised to create) an offence is:

- 'repugnant' if it adds something inconsistent with the provisions of a statute creating the same offence;
- not 'repugnant' by reason only that it adds something not inconsistent with the statute under which it is made: see *Gentel v Rapps* (1902).

Case examples

A by-law purported to impose a penalty on the owner of an animal found straying in a public place unless the owner proved that he or she had taken all reasonable means to prevent the animal from so straying. The by-law was declared invalid because it purported to reverse the onus of proof.

Willoughby Municipal Council v Homer (1926)

A regulation made pursuant to the Transport Act 1930 (NSW) required the driver of a public vehicle to furnish information to an authorised officer when requested to do so. A taxi driver was stopped by an authorised officer and asked if he was engaged in multiple hiring (an offence under another regulation). The driver refused to answer. The court held that a person could be required to supply information, but only in relation to matters actually dealt with in other regulations, and, in any event, the common law privilege against self-incrimination could not, in the absence of express legislative direction, be overridden.

ex p Grinham; Re Sneddon (1961)

A piece of subordinate legislation is:

- not 'repugnant' to the general law merely because it creates a new offence, or because it declares unlawful that which the law does not say is unlawful;
- 'repugnant' to the general law only if it makes unlawful that which the general law says is lawful: see *Gentel v Rapps* (1902).

Improper purpose

A statutory rule may be declared invalid because the power to make the rule has not been exercised for the *proper* purpose.

The *proper* purpose is the purpose for which the power was conferred, whether or not that purpose is set out in the empowering statute.

Any other purpose is an *improper* one.

Case examples

A committee was empowered by statute to regulate all aspects of vegetable seed processing and distribution. The committee allegedly had also set itself up as a seed merchant. It ordered the company, a seed merchant, not to sell certain types of seeds without the committee's approval. The court held that the orders, although ostensibly within the committee's powers, would be void (and could be so declared) if it could be proved that the committee had made them to, for example, reduce its own business competition.

Arthur Yates & Co Pty Ltd v Vegetable Seeds Committee (1945)

A planning regulation describing the area of the town of Darwin as 4,350 sq km (including most of the Cox Peninsula which was, relevantly, the subject of an Aboriginal land claim) was found not to have been made for a town planning purpose.

R v Toohey (Aboriginal Land Commissioner);
ex p Northern Land Council (1981)

Unreasonableness

A statutory rule may be declared invalid if it is 'unreasonable' (or 'irrational').

'Unreasonableness' in administrative law usually means 'manifest unreasonableness', that is, a decision so unreasonable that no reasonable body could have made it: see *Associated Provincial Picture Houses Ltd v Wednesbury Corporation* (1948).

However, in the context of the validity of subordinate legislation, unreasonableness generally means something quite different.

In *Kruse v Johnson* (1898), Lord Russell stated that a by-law would not be unreasonable merely because:

- a reviewing court thought that it went further than was prudent, necessary or convenient; or
- it was not accompanied by a qualification or an exception which the court thought ought to be there,

but would be unreasonable if it:

- was 'partial and unequal' in its operation as between different classes of persons;
- was 'manifestly unjust';
- disclosed bad faith; or
- involved 'such oppressive and gratuitous interference with the rights of those subject to [it] as could find no justification in the minds of reasonable men'.

However, in *Williams v Melbourne Corporation* (1933), Dixon J (as he then was) had this to say about the matter:

> Although in some jurisdictions the unreasonableness of a by-law made under statutory powers by a local governing body is still considered a separate ground of invalidity ... in this court, it is not so treated ...

> To determine whether a by-law is an exercise of a power, it is not always enough to ascertain the subject matter of the power and consider whether the by-law appears on its face to relate to that subject. The true nature and purpose of the power must be determined, and it must often be necessary to examine the operation of the by-law in the local circumstances to which it is intended to apply. Notwithstanding that *ex facie* there seemed a sufficient connection between the subject of the power and that of the by-law, the true character of the by-law may then appear to be

such that *it could not reasonably have been adopted as a means of attaining the ends of the power.* In such a case, the by-law will be invalid, not because it is inexpedient or misguided, but because it is not a real exercise of the power ... [Emphasis added.]

Unreasonableness – at least in the High Court of Australia and most other Australian superior courts – in the context of subordinate legislation:

- is not generally treated as being a separate ground of invalidity in the English sense;
- has a fairly narrow operation;
- refers to a 'purported' and 'not a real' exercise of the delegated law making power such that it could not reasonably have been adopted as a means of attaining the ends of the power.

However, before *Williams v Melbourne Corporation* was decided, the test of 'unreasonableness' in *Kruse v Johnson* had been approved and applied by the Privy Council in *R v Broad* (1915) and was in later High Court cases treated as good law: see, for example, *Brunswick Corporation v Stewart* (1941); *Carter v Egg Marketing Board* (1942). Thus, 'unreasonableness' in the *Kruse v Johnson* sense may be a possible ground of challenge, at least perhaps where the piece of subordinate legislation is a by-law made by a local government authority.

Nevertheless, a wide test of 'unreasonableness' has certainly been rejected in Australia at least insofar as local government authority by-laws are concerned: see, for example, *Jones v Metropolitan Meat Board* (1925).

Lack of proportionality

The European Court of Justice has laid down the principle that, to be valid, subordinate legislation must conform with the so called 'principle of proportionality': see *R v Intervention Board for Agricultural Produce ex p ED & F Man (Sugar) Ltd* (1986).

The principle of proportionality is as follows:

- The means employed by the statutory rule must be 'appropriate and necessary' to attain the authorised object: see *State of New South Wales v Macquarie Bank Ltd* (1992), *per* Kirby P.
- If the burden imposed by the rule is clearly out of proportion to the authorised object, the rule will be invalid.

- There must therefore exist a reasonable relationship, or 'reasonable proportionality', between the end (that is, the exercise of the power) and the means of the law (that is, the means which the law embodies for achieving that purpose), such that:
  - ꞈ the means must be reasonably likely to bring about the apparent objective of the law; and
  - ꞈ the detriment to those adversely affected must not be disproportionate to the benefit to the public envisaged by the legislation: see *Commonwealth v Tasmania* (1983); *State of New South Wales v Macquarie Bank* (1992).
- It is not enough that the court itself considers the rule to be inexpedient or misguided. The rule must be so lacking in reasonable proportionality as 'not to be a real exercise of the power': see *South Australia v Tanner* (1989).

There is some doubt as to whether, in Australian law, lack of proportionality is an independent ground of review of the validity of subordinate legislation: see *Minister for Urban Affairs and Planning v Rosemount Estates Pty Ltd* (1996); *Save the Showground for Sydney Inc v Minister for Urban Affairs and Planning* (1996); cf *South Australia v Tanner* (1989).

In that regard, it is:

- debatable whether, in the context of judicial review of subordinate legislation, lack of proportionality is saying much more than what is already subsumed within other accepted grounds of invalidity: see *Minister for Resources v Dover Fisheries Pty Ltd* (1993);
- difficult to distinguish between what Dixon J in *Williams v Melbourne Corporation* (1933) accepted as the 'unreasonableness' ground of invalidity and what is now being referred to as 'lack of proportionality'.

Both grounds of invalidity speak in terms of:

- 'means' and 'ends'; and
- the purported exercise of power not being a real exercise of power.

Implicit, if not explicit, in each approach is the conclusion that the legislature could not have intended to give authority to make the subordinate legislation in question: cf *Kruse v Johnson* (1898).

One view is that lack of proportionality is merely a sub-ground of irrationality (or manifest unreasonableness): see *Minister for Urban*

Affairs and Planning v Rosemount Estates Pty Ltd (1996), *per* Handley and Cole JJA.

Uncertainty

A statutory rule may be declared invalid on the ground of uncertainty, in the sense that it imposes no certain obligation on the person or persons affected by it.

There is, however, some confusion in the cases as to just what is meant by the term 'uncertainty'.

'Uncertainty' can mean:

- uncertainty *as to result*, such that no reasonable person could comply with the rule: see *Television Corporation Ltd v Commonwealth* (1963);
- uncertainty *as to meaning*, such that the rule cannot be given any meaning, or any sensible or ascertainable meaning: see *Fawcett Properties Ltd v Buckingham County Council* (1961).

There are also two judicial approaches as to the effect of uncertainty:

1   The 'invalidity' approach:

The uncertain rule is declared invalid, in whole or in part.

2   The 'interpretation' approach:

The offending rule, or the offending part of the rule, may not actually be declared invalid if the uncertainty (generally, an ambiguity) can, in the opinion of the reviewing court, be satisfactorily resolved in favour of the person subject to the rule.

Case example

The Prices Commissioner had the power to fix maximum prices for clothing and had made an order relating to men's and boys' clothes. The order did not, however, state amounts in money. The High Court, which invalidated the order on the ground of uncertainty, stated that the Commissioner, in fixing prices, did not actually have to express amounts in money terms. Nevertheless, if the Commissioner chose to use a formula, standard or criteria, it had to be capable of producing a uniform result which every person, given the facts and figures and calculating correctly, would arrive at. The order in question was not capable of being complied with.

King Gee Clothing Co Pty Ltd v Commonwealth (1945)

See, also, *Re Gold Coast City (Touting and Distribution of Printed Matter) Law 1994* (1995).

Sub-delegation

A statutory rule may be declared invalid if the legislative power to make the rule is, in the absence of express authority, purportedly sub-delegated.

The general common law position is summed up in the Latin maxim *delegatus non potest delegare*, that is, a delegate cannot delegate. However, the legislature can, and often does, provide otherwise.

Case example

> The Governor General, who was empowered to fix milk prices, made an order purportedly authorising the minister to fix the town milk producer price. The court held that the Governor General could not validly sub-delegate the very matter entrusted to him for decision. (The court did, however, say that the position may have been different if the Governor General had determined a precise basis or formula upon which the prices were to be determined: cf the *King Gee* case.)
>
> *Hawke's Bay Raw Milk Producers Co-operative Co Ltd*
> *v New Zealand Milk Board* (1961)

In certain jurisdictions, a statutory rule will not offend the rule against sub-delegation where it authorises (pursuant to express statutory authority) some matter or thing to be from time to time determined, applied or regulated by some specified person or body: see s 42(2)(c) of the Interpretation Act 1987 (NSW).

Example

> Assume that a statute enables a regulation to be made fixing the minimum room size for a habitable room in a dwelling-house. A regulation could then be made stating that the minimum room size shall be as determined by the local council.

The regulation/prohibition distinction

A power to 'regulate', or to make a statutory rule 'regulating', some matter, does not, *in itself*, confer power to 'prohibit' that matter:

- either unconditionally (that is, absolutely);

- or conditionally (for example, subject to a discretionary licence or consent being obtained from some person or body): see *Brooks v Selwyn* (1882); *Melbourne Corporation v Barry* (1922); *Swan Hill Corporation v Bradbury* (1937); *Goldberg v Law Institute of Victoria* (1972); *Foley v Padley* (1984).

A statutory rule made under a power to 'regulate':

- may prescribe time, place, manner and circumstance; and
- may impose conditions; but
- must stop short of preventing or suppressing the matter to be regulated: see *Swan Hill Corporation v Bradbury* (1937).

Case example

> A statute enabled by-laws to be made 'regulating or restraining' the erection and construction of buildings. A by-law was made by a local council purporting to prevent a person from erecting or constructing certain types of buildings except with the approval of the council. The by-law was held by the High Court to be invalid.
>
> *Swan Hill Corporation v Bradbury* (1937)

It should, nevertheless, be kept in mind that the legislature can provide otherwise: see (now repealed) s 530 of the Local Government Act 1919 (NSW), which expressly provided that the power to 'regulate' was deemed to confer power to license, prevent or prohibit.

A power to 'prohibit', or to make a statutory rule 'prohibiting', some matter, confers power to prohibit:

- either unconditionally (that is, absolutely);
- or conditionally (for example, subject to a discretionary licence or consent being obtained from some person or body): see *Country Roads Board v Neale Ads Pty Ltd* (1930); *Radio Corporation Pty Ltd v Commonwealth* (1938).

Case example

> A board, which was empowered to make by-laws prohibiting the erection of advertising hoardings in the vicinity of State highways, made a by-law prohibiting the erection of such hoardings except with the consent in writing of the board. The by-law was held by the High Court to be valid.
>
> *Country Roads Board v Neale Ads Pty Ltd* (1930)

It should also be noted that the making of an instrument in those terms does not, in itself, amount to an unlawful delegation of legislative power.

'As if enacted' clauses

Regulation making powers in some statutes contain provisions stating that any regulations made under the relevant statute shall have 'the like force and effect as if they were enacted in this Act'.

An exercise of power under an 'as if enacted' clause will be valid if, in addition to the statutory rule not otherwise being invalid, the rule:

- is one made by the authorities specified in the clause;
- deals with matters specified in the enabling statute and is not inconsistent with the statute; and
- is not patently or absurdly irrelevant to the subject matter of the enabling statute.

See *Foster v Aloni* (1951).

Severance

A statutory rule may be *ultra vires* only in part.

The rules in relation to severance are as follows:

- The courts presume, in the absence of a clear statement of a contrary legislative intention, that the legislature does not intend to give its assent to a partial operation of one of its enactments or instruments: see *Bank of New South Wales v Commonwealth* (1948).
- However, the legislature can provide otherwise. So called 'severability clauses' exist in several jurisdictions: see s 46(b) of the Acts Interpretation Act 1901 (Cth), s 31(2) of the Interpretation Act 1987 (NSW).
- A severability clause:
  - reverses the judicial presumption that the instrument is to operate as a whole; and
  - is construed such that the intention of the legislature is taken *prima facie* to be that:

- – the enactment should be divisible; and
- – any parts found unobjectionable should be carried into effect independently of those which fail: see *Bank of New South Wales*.

- Severance will not, however, be possible where:
  - ○ the invalid provision forms part of an inseparable context: see *Kent County Council v Kingsway Investments (Kent) Ltd* (1971); and *Thames Water Authority v Elmbridge Borough Council* (1983);
  - ○ the rejection of the invalid part of the rule would mean that the otherwise unobjectionable provision would operate differently upon the persons, matters or things falling under it, or in some other way would produce a different result: see *Bank of New South Wales*.

3 Procedural Fairness

You should be familiar with the following areas:

- the hearing rule, the bias rule and the 'no evidence' rule
- the types of cases in which the courts will imply a duty to act fairly
- the circumstances in which the hearing rule may be excluded or displaced or may simply not apply
- the different tests to determine bias

Introduction

> They must be masters of their own procedure. They should be subject to no rules save this: they must be fair ... The public interest demands it.
>
> *Re Pergamon Press Ltd* (1971), *per* Lord Denning MR

Natural justice has a close association with natural law which has a history dating back to the Greeks in the 6th century BC.

Whereas legal positivism asserts that persons possess only those rights that have been granted by human made law, natural law maintains that:

- individuals have certain inalienable human rights which at all times have been reflected in universally accepted standards of justice;
- those standards of justice require some minimum protection of human rights;
- a valid law is one which:
  - conforms to generally accepted standards of reason, reasonableness and justice (that is, 'rational humaneness', to use the words of the 19th century radical John Morley); and

> ◦   does not violate fundamental human rights.

Initially, only courts of law and court-like bodies were required to accord natural justice.

Over the years, the application of the so called rules of natural justice was extended to include those persons, bodies and authorities (whether governmental or not) whose decisions may adversely affect members of the public.

In recent years, many jurists and commentators have come to prefer the term 'procedural fairness' to 'natural justice'.

Indeed, it is now more common to speak of in terms of a 'duty to act fairly' rather than a duty to observe the rules of natural justice.

For the most part, the expressions are interchangeable. However, the term 'procedural fairness' has certain advantages. In that regard, in *Kioa v West* (1985), Mason J (as he then was) said:

> In this respect, the expression 'procedural fairness' more aptly conveys the notion of a flexible obligation to adopt fair procedures which are appropriate and adapted to the circumstances of a particular case. The statutory power must be exercised fairly, that is, in accordance with procedures that are fair to the individual considered in the light of the statutory requirements, the interests of the individual and the interests and purposes, whether public or private, which the statute seeks to advance or protect or permits to be taken into account as legitimate considerations ... .

Where does 'fairness' come from?

One view is that fairness comes from 'religion'. Lord Denning was an exponent of, and believer in, this view. According to Denning (see Iris Freeman, *Lord Denning: A Life*, 1993, London: Hutchinson), the aim of the law is to see that truth is observed and that justice is done between persons. But what is 'truth' and what is 'justice'?

According to Denning, on these two cardinal questions religion and law meet. It is about how the 'right spirit is created in us'. Religion, or rather the Christian religion, is, for Denning, concerned with the creation of that spirit. Where did Denning find his principles of law? From the Christian faith. 'I do not know where else ... to find them', he said in a 1943 BBC Home Service radio broadcast.

Of course, with all due respect to Lord Denning, notions of fairness and natural justice predate Christianity. Unless one interpolates the spiritual notion of an 'anonymous Christ' (cf Catholicism), one cannot, in all good reason, attribute our notions of fairness to Christianity, or any other religion for that matter, although that is not to say that our understanding of, and initiation into, those notions was not rooted in our early faith and conditioning. Even Denning himself admitted:

> The common law of the land has been moulded for centuries by judges who have been brought up in the Christian faith. The precepts of religion, consciously or unconsciously, have been their guide in the administration of justice.

An alternative view is that our sense of fairness and justice is 'innate', and is not inculcated by religion, although it may well be reinforced by it and other conditioning.

In the fourth chapter of *The Descent of Man*, Charles Darwin accumulated examples of co-operative behaviour among social animals, and concluded:

> It can hardly be disputed that the social feelings are instinctive or innate in the lower animals; and why should they not be so in man?

He concluded the chapter with what may be regarded as the classical statement or the humanist view on the social basis of morals:

> The social instincts – the prime principle of man's moral constitution – with the aid of active intellectual powers and the effects of habit, naturally lead to the golden rule. 'As ye would that men should do to you, do ye to them likewise'; and this lies at the foundation of morality.

The rules of procedural fairness

In *Kioa v West* (1985), Mason J (as he then was) stated:

> The law has now developed to a point where it may be accepted that there is a common law duty to act fairly, in the sense of according procedural fairness, in the making of administrative decisions which affect rights, interests and legitimate expectations, subject only to the clear manifestation of a contrary intention.

The rules of procedural fairness are encompassed in very broad terms in three common law rules encompassing minimum standards of fair decision making:

- The *audi alteram partem* (or 'hearing') rule: the right to a fair hearing.
- The *nemo judex* (or 'bias') rule: no one can be judge in his or her own cause.
- The 'no evidence' (or 'probative evidence') rule: decisions must be based upon logically probative material.

Procedural fairness, in the sense of a duty to act fairly, is *implied* at common law in the absence of a clear, unambiguous contrary intention in the legislation or other regulatory instrument governing the making of the particular decision.

In *Kioa v West* (1985), Mason J said:

> It is a fundamental rule of the common law doctrine of natural justice expressed in traditional terms that, generally speaking, when an order is to be made which will deprive a person of some right or interest or the legitimate expectation of a benefit, he is entitled to know the case sought to be made against him and to be given an opportunity of replying to it ...

> The reference to 'right or interest' in this formulation must be understood as relating to personal liberty, status, preservation of livelihood and reputation, as well as to proprietary rights and interests ...

Case example

> The appellants were ordered to be deported. The decision maker had taken into account a departmental submission recommending deportation which contained prejudicial statements (adverse representations) against one of the appellants. The appellants had not been given an opportunity to answer the adverse material. The High Court found that there had been a breach of the rules of procedural fairness by the failure to give the appellants an opportunity to respond to the material prejudicial to them in the submission and ordered that the deportation order be set aside.

Kioa v West (1985)

Deane J in *Kioa* said:

> In the absence of a clear contrary legislative intent, a person who is entrusted with statutory power to make an administrative decision which directly affects the rights, interests, status or legitimate expectations of another in his individual capacity (as distinct from as a member of the general public or of a class of the

general public) is bound to observe the requirements of natural justice or procedural fairness.

It is, however, accepted that the legislature may displace that rule by providing otherwise: see *R v Brixton Prison (Governor) ex p Soblen* (1963); *Salemi v MacKellar (No 2)* (1977); *R v MacKellar ex p Ratu* (1977).

The rules of procedural fairness (natural justice)

1   The *audi alteram partem* [hearing] rule:

The right to a fair hearing.

2   The *nemo judex* [bias] rule:

No one can be a judge in his or her own cause.

3   The 'no evidence' rule:

An administrative decision must be based upon logically probative material.

The hearing rule

Rights

In *Twist v Randwick Municipal Council* (1976), Barwick CJ stated:

> The common law rule that a statutory authority having power to affect the rights of a person is bound to hear him before exercising the power is both fundamental and universal ...

In an oft-cited *dictum*, which has become the *locus classicus* of the legal position in relation to the right to be heard, Byles J in *Cooper v Wandsworth Board of Works* (1863) stated:

> ... although there are no positive words in a statute requiring that the party shall be heard, yet the justice of the common law will supply the omission of the legislature.

The hearing rule:

- is not confined to the conduct of strictly legal tribunals; but
- is applicable to every tribunal or body of persons invested with authority to adjudicate upon matters involving civil consequences to individuals: see *Wood v Woad* (1874); *Municipal Council of Sydney v Harris* (1912); *Ridge v Baldwin* (1964).

However, the application of the hearing rule was greatly, and regrettably, restricted for some 40 years following the decision of the English Court of Appeal in *R v Electricity Commissioners ex p London Electricity Joint Committee Co (1920) Ltd* (1924), where a *dictum* of Atkin LJ was interpreted in such a way as to exclude the right to be heard unless the particular decision being taken:

- affected a person's legal *rights*; and
- was being taken by a body which had a duty to act 'judicially' (that is, a court-like body).

The House of Lords, in the landmark case of *Ridge v Baldwin* (1964), returned to earlier authorities such as *Cooper's* case and re-affirmed the so called 'unbroken line of authority' (*per* Lord Reid).

In *Ridge v Baldwin* (1964) a chief constable had been dismissed from office by a committee without an adequate hearing. The dismissal was found to be null and void. *Ridge's* case was applied by the High Court of Australia in *Banks v Transport Regulation Board (Vic)* (1968).

It is now clear that the critical factor is:

- not the nature of the decision or the decision maker ('judicial', 'quasi-judicial', 'administrative', etc);
- not the form of the particular decision making process; but
- the nature and effect of the particular decision: see *Council of Civil Service Unions v Minister for the Civil Service* (1985); *Minister for Arts, Heritage and Environment v Peko-Wallsend Ltd* (1987).

Interests

In subsequent decisions, the application of the hearing rule was extended to decisions which did not affect a person's legal rights in the strict legal sense: see *Nagle v Feilden* (1966); *Trivett v Nivison* (1976).

In *Banks v Transport Regulation Board (Vic)* (1968) – sometimes referred to as Australia's *Ridge v Baldwin* – the High Court held that the board's revocation of the appellant's taxi-cab licence was in breach of the rules of procedural fairness. Interestingly, and significantly, the actual decision to revoke the licence was made, or at least confirmed, by the governor-in-council. Barwick CJ stated that proceedings of the governor-in-council in performance of a statutory function could be void and in an appropriate case be so declared.

Similarly, in *FAI Insurances Ltd v Winneke* (1982), the High Court held that the relevant statutory power (again that of the governor-in-council) to renew, or not renew, a workers compensation insurer's approval was subject to the requirements of procedural fairness.

Civic office

The rules of procedural fairness have also been held to apply in the context of the holding of civic office.

Thus, in *Durayappah v Fernando* (1967), the Privy Council found that a decision of a minister to dissolve a local council for alleged incompetence had been made in breach of the rules of procedural fairness. The council had not been given the right to be heard in its own defence.

Similarly, in *Balmain Association Inc v The Planning Administrator for the Leichhardt Council* (1991), the NSW Court of Appeal held that the appointment of a planning administrator to a council amounted to disciplinary action which attracted the duty of procedural fairness and a right to be heard before such action was taken: cf *ex p R (ex rel Warringah Shire Council and Jones); Re Barnett* (1967).

Legitimate expectations

In the English Court of Appeal decision of *Schmidt v Secretary of State for Home Affairs* (1969), Lord Denning MR invoked the concept of a 'legitimate expectation' to attract a duty to act fairly in circumstances where, for example, an entry permit is revoked before the time for its expiration.

The concept of a 'legitimate expectation' is a difficult one. For one thing, it is not always clear just what is being legitimately expected.

Thus, in *Schmidt*, Lord Denning spoke of an alien's legitimate expectation of being *allowed to stay* in the country for the permitted time. However, it could equally be said that such a person has a legitimate expectation of being *granted a hearing* in the event that the decision maker intends to revoke the permit before the time for its expiration.

In any event, where there already is a recognised right or interest which attracts a duty to act fairly, the concept of a legitimate expectation appears somewhat unnecessary.

The concept of a legitimate expectation has been a useful judicial means of expanding the scope of the applicability of the rules of procedural fairness. It has, for example, been invoked where:

- The decision maker has given some undertaking or assurance to the person likely to be affected by the decision that he or she would be consulted before any decision was made: see *R v Liverpool Corporation ex p Liverpool Taxi Fleet Operators' Association* (1972).

- The decision maker has a policy or practice whereby it regularly acts in a certain way (for example, gives notice of the receipt of a building application to adjoining landowners and invites submissions).

  The regular application of the policy or practice creates an enforceable legitimate expectation that such notice will be given, and that any representations made will be duly considered before any decision is made: see *AG of Hong Kong v Ng Yuen Shiu* (1983); *Council of Civil Service Unions and Others v Minister for the Civil Service* (1985); *Kioa v West* (1985); *Haoucher v Minister of State for Immigration and Ethnic Affairs* (1990); *Hardi v Woollahra Municipal Council* (1987); *Nelson v Burwood Municipal Council* (1991); *Cooper v Maitland City Council* (1992).

- There is, in existence, some law, convention, treaty or policy (not otherwise displaced by some statutory or executive indication to the contrary) which gives rise to a legitimate expectation that its provisions will be followed or otherwise taken into account in the decision making process: see *Minister for Immigration and Ethnic Affairs v Teoh* (1995).

- The person likely to be affected has an interest which, although not presently classifiable as, and falling short of, a legal right, and not presently held, is nevertheless important enough that some degree of procedural fairness be afforded.

Thus, an applicant for a licence or an approval, who has never held a licence or been granted an approval before, is still entitled to a measure of procedural rectitude (for example, proper consideration and no bias), even though there may not be an actual right to be heard: see *McInnes v Onslow-Fane* (1978); cf *Idonz Pty Ltd v National Capital Development Commission* (1986).

Legitimate expectations must be reasonably based: see *Kioa v West* (1985).

The existence of a legitimate expectation that a decision maker will act in a certain way:

- does not compel a substantive right; but
- affords a right to be heard before a decision is made or action taken: see *Salemi v MacKellar (No 2)* (1977); *AG for the State of NSW v Quin* (1989); *Save the Showground for Sydney Inc v Minister for Urban Affairs and Planning* (1996);
- does not necessarily compel the decision maker to act in that way, but if the decision maker proposes to make a decision inconsistent with the legitimate expectation, the person affected must be afforded procedural fairness (that is, be given notice and an adequate opportunity of presenting his or her case): see *Minister of State for Immigration and Ethnic Affairs v Teoh* (1995).

However, a legitimate expectation of being heard:

- does not arise in relation to the exercise of every executive power: see *Save the Showground for Sydney Inc v Minister for Urban Affairs and Planning* (1996); and
- may be excluded by the clear and unambiguous legislative (or other) expression of a contrary intention: see *Medway v Minister for Planning* (1993).

Where, for example, the persons relevantly affected are numerous or difficult to identify (either at present or in advance), such a contrary intention will be more readily inferred: see *Essex County Council v Ministry of Housing and Local Government* (1967); *Bates v Lord Hailsham* (1972); *Medway* (1993); *Botany Bay City Council v Minister for Transport and Regional Development* (1996); *Save the Showground for Sydney Inc v Minister for Urban Affairs and Planning* (1996).

A legitimate expectation arising under a policy (for example, to the effect that consultation will take place before a decision is made or action is otherwise taken):

- can only be based upon the current policy;
- may be affected when the policy is substituted by a new policy and does not itself prevent the adoption of any such new policy: see *Quin* (1989); and
- will be extinguished upon the adoption of a new policy inconsistent with the legitimate expectation based on the old policy: see *In re Findlay and Others* (1985); *AG for the State of NSW v Quin* (1989); *Save the Showground for Sydney Inc v Minister for Urban Affairs and Planning* (1996).

In *Re Minister for Immigration and Multicultural Affairs ex p Lam* (2003), the High Court of Australia considered and qualified the operation of its earlier decision in *Teoh*. In that case, the applicant, whose permanent visa had been cancelled by the respondent on character grounds, was a father. An officer of the respondent asked, by letter, for details of the carers of the children, indicating that the respondent wished to contact them. The applicant provided the details but the carers were never contacted. The applicant sought to establish that he had been denied procedural fairness on the basis that the letter created a legally enforceable 'legitimate expectation', and fairness required that the procedure foreshadowed in the letter should not be departed from without the applicant being informed of the intention to do so. However, the court disagreed, stating that what must be demonstrated is 'unfairness', not merely some departure from a representation. Not every departure from a stated intention necessarily involves unfairness, even if it defeats an expectation. The ultimate question remains whether there has been unfairness, *not* whether an expectation has been disappointed.

Preliminary and staged decision making

There have been cases where the courts have held that the rules of procedural fairness were not implied in relation to the making of what may be termed 'preliminary decisions'.

In many cases, the so called decisions were nothing more than recommendations or conclusions in a report: see *Testro Bros Pty Ltd v Tait* (1963); cf *In re Pergamon Press Ltd* (1971).

Nevertheless, the point has now been reached where, generally speaking, there would seem to be no difference in principle as to the observance of the requirements of procedural fairness between so called final decisions and those which are only preliminary: see *Wiseman v Borneman* (1971); *Lewis v Heffer* (1978).

Where a decision making process involves different stages or steps before a final decision is made:

- The requirements of procedural fairness are ordinarily satisfied if the decision making process, viewed in its entirety, accords procedural fairness: see *South Australia v O'Shea* (1987); cf *Rees v Crane* (1994).

- A right to be heard later will not 'cure' a lack or deficiency of procedural fairness unless:

    o   the steps or stages in the decision making process; and

    o   the various persons and bodies involved in that process

    all form part of the one decision making process: see *Ainsworth v Criminal Justice Commission* (1992); *Johns v Australian Securities Commission* (1993).

- It is not always sufficient to say that if the rules of procedural fairness apply to the procedure as a whole they do not have to be followed in any individual stage.

- The question always remains in every case whether fairness requires that a hearing be given at, relevantly, a preliminary stage: see *Rees v Crane* (1994).

- There is no absolute rule that procedural fairness need not be observed at one stage of a procedure if there is to be, under the procedure, an opportunity to be heard later, particularly so where the relevant legislation is silent as to the procedure to be followed at each stage: see *Rees*.

- As a matter of statutory construction and interpretation, legislation providing for an opportunity to be heard later is not to be construed as necessarily excluding a right to be informed and heard at the first or earlier stage: see *Rees*.

In *Rees v Crane* (1994), the Privy Council said:

> ... there may be situations in which natural justice does not require that a person must be told of the complaints made against him and given a chance to answer them at the particular stage in question. Essential features leading the courts to this conclusion have included the fact that the investigation is purely preliminary, that there will be a full chance adequately to deal with the complaints later, that the making of the inquiry without observing the *audi alteram partem* maxim is justified by urgency or administrative necessity, that no penalty or serious damage to reputation is inflicted by proceeding to the next stage without

such preliminary notice, that the statutory scheme properly construed excludes such a right to know and to reply at the earlier stage.

However, their Lordships went on to state that:

- There was no absolute rule to that effect, even if there was to be, under the procedure, an opportunity to answer the charges later.
- The existence of an opportunity to be heard later is a pointer in favour of the general practice but it is not conclusive.

As to an opportunity to be heard at a preliminary stage:

- As a matter of statutory interpretation, statutory silence (as to any right to be heard at such a stage) is not to be construed as necessarily excluding a right to be informed and heard at that stage: see *Rees*.
- A hearing at that stage may, however, defeat the legislative intent and be contrary to the public interest.
- Indeed, where the legislation makes express provision for a right to be heard at a later stage, and the earlier stage or stages are only (and truly) preliminary, a court may well hold that there is no duty to afford procedural fairness at the earlier stage or stages: see *Medway v Minister for Planning* (1993).

Exclusion or displacement of the hearing rule

The common law implied 'duty to act fairly' can be excluded or otherwise displaced, as follows:

- The legislature may exclude or displace the hearing rule by making provision for the exercise of a power without a hearing being afforded to the affected party: see *Twist v Randwick Municipal Council* (1976).
- If, however, the legislature intends to dispense with the requirements of procedural fairness in a particular enactment, that intention must be 'unambiguously clear': see *Twist, per* Barwick CJ.
- Such a legislative intention is not to be assumed, nor is it spelled out from indirect references, uncertain inferences or equivocal considerations, but must satisfactorily appear from express words of plain intendment: see *Commissioner of Police v Tanos* (1958).

- Nor is such an intention to be inferred from the presence in the statute of rights commensurate with some of the rules of procedural fairness: see *Annetts v McCann* (1990).

Case example

> The appellant was served with an order under s 317B of the Local Government Act 1919 (NSW) to demolish his house unless it was restored to the respondent council's satisfaction within a reasonable time. The legislation gave a right of appeal to the District Court of NSW against the order, but the appellant chose not to exercise that right. He was given an extension of time to comply with the order, but he failed to comply. The council then resolved to execute the order. The appellant sought to argue that before issuing the demolition order the council was bound by the rules of procedural fairness to have given him an opportunity to be heard on the question of whether such an order should be made. The High Court held that the legislature, in enacting s 317B (with its right of appeal to a court), had provided an opportunity for the owner of a property to be heard before that person's rights were finally affected.

Twist v Randwick Municipal Council (1976)

As regards private clubs and associations, the preferable view in Australia is that natural justice comes to operate in such private bodies by the rules of those bodies (implied terms) on the basis that fair procedures are intended, but recognising the possibility that express words or necessary implication in the rules could exclude natural justice in whole or in part: see *Dickason v Edwards* (1910); *McClelland v Burning Palms Surf Life Saving Club* (2002). In that regard, there would not appear to be any general rule of public policy that would operate so as to prevent the rules of natural justice from being ousted by an express term which excludes them.

The mere existence of a right of appeal may not in some circumstances satisfy the requirements of natural justice: see *Twist*.

The position now appears to have been reached where the existence of a statutory right of review or appeal:

- may affect the nature of the procedures which ought to be adopted in complying with the hearing rule; but
- ordinarily will not exclude those procedures: see *Marine Hull & Liability Insurance Co Ltd v Hurford and Another* (1985).

Various other factors such as urgency:

- may also diminish the content of the hearing rule; but
- will not necessarily exclude or displace the rule altogether: see *Tanos* (1958); *Durayappah v Fernando* (1967); *Heatley v Tasmanian Racing and Gaming Commission* (1977); *Dixon v Commonwealth* (1981); *Marine Hull*.

For a recent case concerning the question of statutory exclusion of the right to be heard, see *Re Minister for Immigration and Multicultural Affairs ex p Miah* (2001).

The nature of the power being exercised (for example, a power to suspend a person from duty pending inquiries) may, in some cases, be such that the power may be exercised peremptorily, without a hearing first being afforded the affected person: see *Lewis v Heffer* (1978); *Furnell v Whangarei High Schools Board* (1973); *Dixon* (1981).

Such a course of action should, however, be followed only in exceptional or special cases of exigency and the action taken should be of short duration: see *Tanos*; *Heatley*.

Non-application of the hearing rule

It is somewhat dangerous to even entertain the possibility that there may still be some cases where the hearing rule does not apply.

Indeed, in any event, to the extent to which there may be such a case, it may be preferable to speak in terms of the hearing rule having little or no 'work' to do or the content of the rule being reduced to 'nothingness' (see below).

Be that as it may, the courts do, from time to time, speak in terms of the hearing rule having no application to the facts of a particular case.

This *may* occur where:

- The decision is seen by the reviewing court as being, in effect, 'purely administrative'.

  However, even then there is almost invariably some 'policy' or other critical factor involved (for example, the conduct of the affected party militates against the provision of a hearing in the circumstances of the particular case: see *Lovelock v Secretary of State for Transport* (1979); *Cinnamond v British Airport Authority* (1980).

- The decision (for example, to dismiss a person from employment) occurs in the context of a straightforward master-servant relationship: see *Ridge v Baldwin* (1964), *per* Lord Reid.

However, a right to be heard will readily be implied into a statutory framework. 'Unfair dismissal' laws may also alter the legal position. In that regard, the rights of an employee to be consulted before dismissal (now embodied in legislation: see, for example, s 170DC of the Workplace Relations Act 1996 (Cth)) have been well established: see, for example, *Gregory v Philip Morris Ltd* (1988); *Wheeler v Philip Morris Ltd* (1988); *Byrne v Australian Airlines Ltd* (1976). Ordinarily, before being dismissed, the employee must be made aware of the particular matters that are putting his or her job at risk and given an adequate opportunity of defence: see, for example, *Nicolson v Heaven & Earth Gallery Pty Ltd* (1994); *Gibson v Bosmac Pty Ltd* (1995); cf *Selvachandran v Peteron Plastics Pty Ltd* (1995).

• The decision affects so many people that it is tantamount to a legislative act.

For example, the rules of procedural fairness were held to have no application in relation to the designation of a third London airport: see *Essex County Council v Ministry of Housing and Local Government* (1967) and a decision to exempt certain activities in relation to Sydney airport from environmental assessment laws: see *Botany Bay City Council v Minister for Transport and Regional Development* (1996). See also *Re Gosling* (1943), in which it was held that a power to fix milk prices, after holding either a public or private inquiry, was a delegated legislative power in respect of which the rules of procedural fairness had no application.

• The decision occurs in the context of a so called 'application case', that is, where a person makes an application for a licence or an approval of some kind: see *McInnes v Onslow-Fane* (1978).

However, this proposition has to be expressed guardedly as a 'pure applicant' is still entitled to be treated 'fairly' and to be afforded a measure of procedural rectitude (for example, proper consideration and no bias) in the making of the decision, even though there may be no formal right to be heard as such, except perhaps in response to any submissions or objections made by others: see *Perron v Central Land Council* (1985).

• The decision involves so called 'national security' considerations: see *Council of Civil Service Unions v Minister for the Civil Service* (1985). However, it is probably more accurate to say that, in such cases, the right to be heard is overridden by the national security considerations.

Requirements of a 'fair hearing'

The critical question in most cases is not whether the rules of procedural fairness apply, but what does the duty to act fairly require in the circumstances of the particular case? See *Kioa v West* (1985), *per* Mason J.

It has been said that 'the contents of natural justice range from a full blown trial into nothingness': see Johnson, G, 'Natural justice and legitimate expectation in Australia' (1985) 15 FL Rev 39 at 71.

The rules of procedural fairness have a flexible quality and are 'chameleon-like': see *Kioa v West* (1985), *per* Brennan J.

As to the legal requirements of a 'fair hearing':

- The requirements depend on the circumstances of the case, the nature of the inquiry, the rules under which the tribunal is acting, the subject matter that is being dealt with, etc: see *Russell v Duke of Norfolk* (1949); *Kioa v West* (1985).

- The giving of notice is the minimum content of the rules of procedural fairness: see *R v North ex p Oakey* (1927). The hearing will not be a fair one if the person affected is not told the case against him or her: see *R v Gaming Board for Great Britain ex p Benaim and Khaida* (1970).

- The recipient of the notice must be given sufficient information so as to know the critical issues of fact on the basis of which the proposed decision is to be made.

- The decision maker 'need not quote chapter and verse ... [a]n outline of the charge will usually suffice': see *In re Pergamon Press Ltd* (1971), *per* Lord Denning MR.

- Information in the notice must not be vague or general, but complete (even if concisely worded) and in intelligible language: see *Re Palmer and Minister for the Capital Territory* (1978).

- Whatever standard is adopted, one essential is that the person concerned should have a reasonable opportunity of presenting his or her case: see *Russell v Duke of Norfolk* (1949).

- Ordinarily, a hearing does not have to be oral. An opportunity to make written submissions will usually be sufficient: see *Wiseman v Borneman* (1971); *White v Ryde Municipal Council* (1977).

- Where, however, an oral hearing is required:
  -) It must be afforded on all parts of the 'case': see *Hall v NSW Trotting Club Ltd* (1976).

- ⊃ Adequate notice of the time and place of the hearing, and the issues to be considered, must be given so that a reasonable opportunity is provided to prepare for the hearing: see *Ridge v Baldwin* (1964); *R v Thames Magistrates ex p Polemis* (1974).

- ⊃ The decision maker ordinarily does not have to provide the procedural safeguards of a trial.

- ⊃ Any decision to grant or refuse an adjournment is reviewable for denial of procedural fairness, but only if that decision is unreasonable: see *Connelly v Department of Local Government* (1985).

- Where an oral hearing is not required, a reasonable time must be given for the making of any written submissions and representations.

- The decision maker must act in good faith and listen fairly to the other party – 'that is a duty lying upon everyone who decides anything': see *Board of Education v Rice* (1911), *per* Lord Loreburn LC.

- An opportunity must be given to the person likely to be affected to correct or contradict any relevant statement prejudicial to that person: see *Board of Education v Rice* (1911).

- Where it is proposed to make adverse comments about the person in a report or submission recommending some adverse or potentially adverse action, the person must first be given the opportunity to comment on, or 'rebut', the allegations: see *In re Pergamon Press Ltd* (1971); *Kioa v West* (1985).

- Even where an oral hearing has been given, the person ought to be given a fair opportunity to respond to any adverse finding or conclusion in respect of which the person had not previously been afforded such an opportunity: see *Dainford Ltd v ICAC* (1990).

There is no absolute entitlement to legal representation: see *McNab v Auburn Soccer Sports Club Ltd* (1975); *Finch v Goldstein* (1981); *Krstic v Australian Telecommunications Commission* (1988); *National Crime Authority v A* (1988); *NSW v Canellis* (1994); *McClelland v Burning Palms Surf Life Saving Club* (2002).

However, there may well be cases where procedural fairness will not be satisfied without the granting of legal representation: see *McNab*; *Canellis*; *McClelland*. The courts will have regard to such factors as:

- The legislative intention upon construction of the empowering legislation.

- Whether or not questions of law are involved: see *White v Ryde Municipal Council* (1977).

- A person's capacity to personally represent his or her interests effectively.

  Relevant matters will include the person's familiarity with the relevant 'legal rules' (both substantive and procedural), language difficulties, physical or mental disability, the seriousness of the issue, and so forth: see *Cains v Jenkins* (1979).

Even where there is express statutory provision for a measure of procedural fairness, there is a growing tendency (despite some earlier authorities to the contrary, for example *Twist v Randwick Municipal Council* (1976)) to construe statutory hearing procedures as simply reflecting the intention that procedural fairness is implied and confirming its common law content: see *Marine Hull & Liability Insurance Co Ltd v Hurford* (1985); *Queensland Medical Laboratory v Blewett* (1988); *Busby v Chief Manager, Human Resources Department, Australian Telecommunications Commission* (1988).

In that regard, the fact that the legislation contains some provisions 'commensurate with some of the rules of natural justice' does not necessarily exclude or displace a wider application of those rules in a particular context: see *Annetts v McCann* (1990); cf *Valley Watch Inc v Minister for Planning* (1994).

Thus, even where a minimum content of procedural fairness is afforded by the particular statute, the court may supplement the procedure laid down by the legislature if it is clear that the statutory procedure is insufficient to achieve justice: see *Wiseman v Borneman* (1971); *Annetts v McCann* (1990); cf *Twist* (1976).

The effect of a breach of the hearing rule is as follows:

- The decision is invalid (void, rather than voidable): see *Ridge v Baldwin* (1964).

- Although the decision may ultimately be declared void by the court, the fact that it has been 'made' still gives the court jurisdiction to hear an appeal against it (in the event of there being a statutory right of appeal): see *Calvin v Carr* (1979).

The bias rule

The second rule of procedural fairness is the so called 'bias rule', the Latin term for which is *nemo debet esse judex in propria causa*, that is, no one can be judge in his or her own cause.

In *R v Sussex Justices ex p McCarthy* (1924), Lord Hewart CJ stated that it was 'of fundamental importance that justice should not only be done, but should manifestly and undoubtedly be seen to be done'.

As with the hearing rule, the bias rule can be displaced by the clear manifestation of a contrary legislative intention: see *Mersey Docks Trustees v Gibbs* (1866); *Jeffs v New Zealand Dairy Production and Marketing Board* (1967).

Three tests have been propounded and applied by the courts over the years to determine whether a decision maker is disqualified from dealing with a particular matter:

- the 'real likelihood' of bias test;
- the 'reasonable suspicion' (or 'reasonable apprehension') of bias test;
- the 'actual' bias test.

Real likelihood of bias test

The 'real likelihood' of bias test had its origins in the decision of *R v Rand* (1866).

Case example

> A council made a claim to acquire certain waterworks. Council bonds, charging the borough fund, were held by a hospital and a friendly society. Two of the justices who adjudicated on the claim were among the trustees in whose name the bonds were held by the two institutions. The court held that there was no real likelihood of bias.
>
> *R v Rand* (1866)

The test was applied by the High Court of Australia in several cases, including *R v Australian Stevedoring Industry Board ex p Melbourne Stevedoring Co Pty Ltd* (1953). A delegate of the board held an inquiry as to whether an employer was fit to continue to be registered as an employer. Prior to the hearing, the delegate made certain remarks which tended to suggest that he had prejudged the matter. The court, holding that it could not be said that the delegate had so conducted himself as to raise a sufficient case of bias, said:

> Bias must be 'real'. The officer must so have conducted himself that a high probability arises of bias inconsistent with the fair performance of his duties, with the result that a substantial distrust of the result must exist in the minds of reasonable persons.

Reasonable suspicion (apprehension) of bias test

The 'reasonable suspicion' (now more commonly referred to as 'reasonable apprehension') of bias test had its origins in the House of Lords' decision in *Dimes v Proprietors of the Grand Junction Canal* (1852).

Case example

> A public company acquired land to construct a canal. Dimes, who had an interest in the subject land, ejected the owners of the company. The company's title to the land was subsequently confirmed by the Vice Chancellor who injuncted Dimes from blocking the canal. The Lord Chancellor, who owned shares in the company, confirmed the Vice Chancellor's actions. The House of Lords held that the Vice Chancellor's orders were not affected by the disqualification of the Lord Chancellor.

> *Dimes v Proprietors of the Grand Junction Canal* (1852)

The reasonable suspicion (apprehension) test was applied by the High Court of Australia as early as 1910, in *Dickason v Edwards*, and has been applied in numerous cases since: see *R v Commonwealth Conciliation and Arbitration Commission ex p The Angliss Group* (1969); *R v Watson ex p Armstrong* (1976); and *Re Media, Entertainment and Arts Alliance ex p The Hoyts Corporation* (1994).

Whether there is a 'real likelihood' or 'reasonable apprehension' of bias is to be assessed through the eyes of a disinterested observer (reasonable person) rather than those of the reviewing court.

'Real likelihood' or 'reasonable apprehension'?

In practice, the two tests will often lead to the same result, but they are not the same (despite the attempt by Lord Denning in *Metropolitan Properties Co (FGC) Ltd v Lannon* (1969) to combine them): cf *R v Sussex Justices ex p McCarthy* (1924), and *R v Camborne Justices ex p Pearce* (1955).

Case examples

> A magistrates' clerk retired with the bench while they were considering their verdict in a case of dangerous driving. The clerk belonged to a firm of solicitors acting in civil proceedings on behalf of the other party to the accident out of which the criminal proceedings arose. The defendant's conviction was quashed, on the ground that there had been a reasonable suspicion of bias.
>
> *R v Sussex Justices ex p McCarthy* (1924)

> A local council had laid an information against the applicant. After hearing the evidence the magistrates retired. The clerk, a member of the council (but not of the council committee which had brought the prosecution), was called in to provide advice on a matter of law. It was held that there was no real likelihood of bias.
>
> *R v Camborne Justices ex p Pearce* (1955)

The 'real likelihood' test tends to denote the *predominant probability* of the risk of bias as discerned by the disinterested observer.

The 'reasonable apprehension' test ordinarily denotes a *substantial possibility* of the risk of bias, once again as discerned by the disinterested observer.

The knowledge to be imputed to the disinterested observer is knowledge of all relevant objective facts (for example, as to the nature of the relationship between the parties, the nature of the particular interest, etc), but not so called 'inside knowledge' (for example, as to the character of the decision maker, or what was actually discussed 'behind closed doors'): see *Hannam v Bradford Corporation* (1970); *Stollery v Greyhound Racing Control Board* (1972).

The 'reasonable apprehension' of bias test is presently favoured in both Australia and England, although the 'real likelihood' of bias test is still occasionally invoked in circumstances where, for whatever reason, the court regards a less strict test of bias as appropriate.

Actual bias test

A more lenient test of 'actual bias' has been applied in relation to the proceedings and decision making of so called domestic tribunals (sporting clubs, etc) and collegiate bodies such as local government authorities.

In *Maloney v New South Wales National Coursing Association Ltd* (1978), the NSW Court of Appeal held that certain proceedings of a disciplinary committee of the respondent association (which had resolved to expel the appellant from the association) were not vitiated by the presence of a person upon the committee who had previously displayed animosity towards the appellant.

The court held that:

- Generally speaking, a mere suspicion of bias will not operate to disqualify a member of a domestic tribunal from dealing with a matter. If it did, the enforcement of consensual rules would be unworkable.

- Where, as was the case with the association in question, there is no separation of adjudicative (judicial) and executive functions, a reasonable apprehension of bias will not be sufficient to disqualify a member of a domestic tribunal.

The decision in *Maloney* has received much criticism: see Tracey, RRS, 'Bias and non-statutory administrative bodies – a wrong turning' (1983) 57 ALJ 80.

However, the position is otherwise with respect to the actual *conduct* of the proceedings themselves. In that regard:

- The 'reasonable apprehension' of bias test will apply to the conduct of the proceedings of a domestic tribunal, that is, to matters of misconduct, impropriety or denials of procedural fairness occurring during the course of the proceedings.

- The test of actual bias *only* applies to disqualifying conduct preceding the actual proceedings: see *Dale v New South Wales Trotting Club Ltd* (1978).

- A test of actual bias (or something quite analogous) has also been applied in the context of collegiate decision making by local government authorities and ministerial and departmental decision making (so called 'departmental bias'): see *Anderton v Auckland City Council* (1978). In that regard:

    o the test would appear to be whether the authority's mind was 'so foreclosed that [it] gave no genuine consideration' to the matter under consideration: see *Franklin v Minister of Town and Country Planning* (1948), *per* Lord Thankerton. See also *Steeples v Derbyshire County Council* (1985) and *R v Amber Valley District Council ex p Jackson* (1985).

- The position, however, may well be otherwise where the decision of the collegiate body is vitiated due to bias on the part of a particular member: see *R v West Coast Council ex p The Strahan Motor Inn* (1995). In such a case:

- ꞌ actual bias need not be proved;
- ꞌ the relevant test would appear to be whether the member unequivocally committed himself or herself to a position such that a reasonable bystander could not but apprehend bias.

- The test of bias, in any event, must be applied realistically when dealing with the conduct and decisions of councillors and ministers who:
  - ꞌ are often placed in a situation in which they must inevitably incline toward confirming their own provisional views;
  - ꞌ often have, and may be expected to support, strong personal views as to what ought to occur in the best interests of the community or the general public;
  - ꞌ cannot be subjected to the rigorous standards of impartiality imposed on judicial officers and members of statutory tribunals.

The 'no evidence' rule

A decision maker must make a decision on the basis of logically probative material rather than mere speculation or suspicion: see *Ashbridge Investments Ltd v Minister of Housing and Local Government* (1965); *Coleen Properties Ltd v Minister of Housing and Local Government* (1971); *Minister for Immigration and Ethnic Affairs v Pochi* (1980); *Mahon v Air New Zealand Ltd* (1984); *Australian Broadcasting Tribunal v Bond* (1990).

This is known as the 'no evidence' rule (or 'probative evidence' rule).

The reviewing court:

- can receive evidence to show what material was before the decision maker when the decision was made; but
- cannot receive evidence so as to decide the matter *de novo*: see *Ashbridge Investments Ltd v Minister of Housing and Local Government* (1965).

Diplock LJ in *R v Deputy Industrial Injuries Commissioner ex p Moore* (1965) said:

> The requirement that a person exercising quasi-judicial functions must base his decision on evidence means no more than it must be based upon material which tends logically to show the existence or non-existence of facts relevant to the issue to be determined, or to show the likelihood or unlikelihood of the occurrence of some future event the occurrence of which would be relevant. It means that he must not spin a coin or consult an astrologer, but he may take into account any material which, as a matter of reason, has some probative value in the sense mentioned above. If it is capable of having any probative value, the weight to be attached to it is a matter for the person to whom Parliament has entrusted the responsibility of deciding the issue ... .

'No evidence' means just that – no probative evidence properly before the decision maker: see *Australian Broadcasting Tribunal v Bond* (1990), *per* Deane J. Thus, so long as there is some basis for, say, an inference of fact, there is no place for judicial review on 'no evidence' grounds.

'Duty' to initiate inquiries

A decision maker is not ordinarily under any legal duty to initiate inquiries.

The general principle is as follows:

- Any so called duty to initiate inquiries ordinarily extends to only those matters which are known to the decision maker.

- Ordinarily, those matters should be notified to the decision maker by the party who relies upon them (for example, the applicant for development consent). In other words, the obligation of consideration is more passive than active: see *Hospital Action Group Association Inc v Hastings Municipal Council* (1993), and *Byron Shire Businesses for the Future Inc v Byron Council* (the *Club Med* case) (1994).

- To that extent there is no obligation on the decision maker:

  o   to initiate inquiries: see *Minister for Aboriginal Affairs v Peko-Wallsend Ltd* (1986); or

  o   to give a person advance notice that a submission or an application is insufficiently persuasive to warrant a favourable decision or determination: see *Barina Corporation v Deputy Commissioner of Taxation (NSW)* (1985).

- Where, however, it is obvious that material is readily available which is centrally relevant to the decision to be made, and the decision maker fails to initiate inquiries, the decision may be susceptible to being struck down on the grounds of manifest unreasonableness: see *Prasad v Minister for Immigration and Ethnic Affairs* (1985).
- A decision maker may also act unlawfully by not making further inquiries where the available material contains some obvious omission or obscurity: see *Videto v Minister for Immigration and Ethnic Affairs (No 2)* (1985).

Case example

> A council granted development consent for a large tourist development. The development application before the council disclosed the fact that approximately 33 species of endangered fauna were likely to be within or near the site of the proposed development. Proceedings challenging the validity of the consent were instituted. The court held that the information on fauna impact before the council was insufficient. Accordingly, it was not reasonably open to the council to conclude that there was not likely to be a significant effect on the environment of endangered fauna. This invalidated the very foundation of the council's decision making process. The consent was struck down by the court.
>
> *Byron Shire Businesses for the Future Inc v Byron Council* (the *Club Med* case) (1994)

The result of not making further inquiries is that the decision maker:

- cannot raise the defence that it was unaware of the matter and unable for that reason to consider it or to appropriately condition the decision or determination; and
- is taken to have constructive or deemed knowledge of the matter in question which ought to have been taken into account in the decision making process.

In *Parramatta City Council v Hale* (1982), it was suggested that local councils would be well advised to gather information themselves, or at least through their officers, where this would not otherwise be available to them, particularly in relation to technical or otherwise controversial matters. This is especially important where a council proposes to make a decision which many would regard as a 'bad' decision.

As to constructive or deemed knowledge:

- Relevant material in the possession of officers, even if never brought to the attention of the person or persons making the actual decision, can be treated as being in the possession of the decision maker: see *Minister for Aboriginal Affairs v Peko-Wallsend Ltd* (1986), *per* Gibbs CJ.

- A decision maker may be deemed to know of relevant information which, even innocently, it has dissuaded or discouraged a person from providing: see *Videto v Minister for Immigration and Ethnic Affairs (No 2)* (1985).

In deciding whether a decision maker has properly taken account of prescribed relevant considerations, the court:

- will look to see whether there was adequate material before it on which to base a proper assessment: see *Darlinghurst Residents' Association v Elarosa Investments Pty Ltd and South Sydney City Council (No 2)* (1992); but

- cannot receive evidence so as to decide the whole matter *de novo*: see *Ashbridge Investments Ltd v Minister of Housing and Local Government* (1965).

'Duty' to give reasons

In the absence of an obligation imposed by statute, an administrative decision maker is under no general duty under the common law to give reasons for its decision: see *Public Service Board v Osmond* (1986).

However, even where there is no express legal duty to give reasons:

- A duty to give reasons might still be implied in some circumstances: see *Osmond*.

- Failure to give reasons (or adequate reasons) may invite a reviewing court to infer that the decision maker had no good reason for the decision and had therefore acted in abuse of power (for example, manifest unreasonableness, no evidence): see *Padfield v Minister of Agriculture, Fisheries and Food* (1968); *Congreve v Home Office* (1976); *Secretary of State for Education and Science v Tameside Metropolitan Borough Council* (1977); *Osmond*.

4 *Ultra Vires*

Introduction

In the mid-19th century, the doctrine of *ultra vires* ('beyond power') became a means of ensuring that executive and administrative authorities (particularly local government authorities) acted within their powers.

Where a decision maker is exercising a power, a superior court has the power to review the exercise of that power to ensure that the decision maker has not gone outside the limits of the power, or otherwise abused the power, and acted *ultra vires*.

The doctrine of *ultra vires* has two limbs:

(a) simple (or narrow) *ultra vires*;
(b) extended (or broad) *ultra vires*.

Simple *ultra vires* has, itself, two limbs:

(a) substantive *ultra vires* (including so called 'implied *ultra vires*');
(b) procedural *ultra vires*.

Extended *ultra vires* also has two limbs:

(a) abuse of power;
(b) failure to exercise power.

Abuse of power covers:

- bad faith;
- improper purpose;
- irrelevant considerations;
- manifest unreasonableness;
- lack of proportionality;
- uncertainty;
- no evidence.

Failure to exercise power covers:

- fettering discretion;
- acting on a policy;
- acting under dictation;
- sub-delegation;
- estoppel.

Simple *ultra vires*

Substantive *ultra vires*

A decision maker must not act in excess of its express power. If it purports to do so, its decision will be void.

However, in *Attorney General v Great Eastern Railway Co* (1880), Lord Selborne stated that:

> ... whatever may fairly be regarded as incidental to, or consequent upon, those things which the Legislature has authorised, ought not (unless expressly prohibited) be held, by judicial construction, to be *ultra vires*.

Again, in *AG v Fulham Corporation* (1921), Sargant J said that a local authority was entitled to do:

> ... not only that which it is expressly authorised, but that which is reasonably incidental to, or consequential upon, that which is in terms authorised.

Case examples

> A council, which was expressly empowered by statute to run tramways, acquired the business of a company which worked

tramways and ran bus services. It was held that the council was acting *ultra vires* in running buses.

London County Council v AG (1902)

A council had statutory power to 'establish baths, wash-houses and open bathing places'. It was held that the power did not authorise the establishment of a municipal laundry.

AG v Fulham Corporation (1921)

A council had set up a department to supply all of its printing and stationery requirements. It was held that such action was *intra vires* on the ground that it could be regarded as incidental to the council's normal functions.

AG v Smethwick Corporation (1932)

A council had statutory power to provide 'for the health of residents in the municipal district'. It was held that the power did not authorise fluoridation of the water supply.

Kerlberg v City of Sale (1964)

A council had statutory power to do 'all things necessary from time to time for the promotion and preservation of public health safety and convenience'. It was held that the power did not permit the council to 'censor' advertisements for products such as tobacco and alcohol.

Pacific Outdoor Advertising Pty Ltd v North Sydney Municipal Council (1979)

The doctrine of *ultra vires* (in its simple or narrow form) must nevertheless be reasonably, and not unreasonably, understood and applied (see *AG v Great Eastern Rly Co* (1880)), particularly where it is clear that the legislature's intention is to confer wide powers in general terms.

However, even where there is no exact limit of power, the courts may still 'imply' limitations on the scope of the general power having regard to, among other things, the nature of the decision maker. This is sometimes referred to as 'implied *ultra vires*'.

Thus, otherwise wide powers of a local government authority may, for example, be read so as not to go beyond the accepted notions of local government or the matters of proper concern to councils: see *Lynch v Brisbane City Council* (1961); *Hazell v Hammersmith and Fulham London Borough Council* (1991).

Case examples

A local council decided to adopt a policy that only petrol pumps of Australian manufacture would be permitted within its local government area. The court held that in matters affecting the good government of its area the council was entitled to act as it thought best in the public interest. However, the court went on to say that there were many considerations of public interest with which a council had 'no concern' and which could not properly enter into the exercise of its discretion. The question whether the policy should be adopted was held to be one of 'general interest' to be dealt with by the legislature of the country.

Re Randwick Municipal Council ex p SF Bowser & Co (1927)

A city council had power to make ordinances for, among other things, the 'good government of the City and the wellbeing of its inhabitants'. The council made an ordinance which provided that a person must not use a stall on any land for the sale or display of goods except pursuant to a licence granted under the ordinance. The High Court of Australia held that the ordinance was valid, but warned that, although the 'good government' ordinance making power was very wide, and expressed no exact limit of power, it would not be read as if it were designed to confide to the city more than matters of local government. The power, the court said, was not to be read as going 'beyond the accepted notions of local government'.

Lynch v Brisbane City Council (1960)

Procedural *ultra vires*

In addition to the substantive limitations imposed upon a decision maker's powers, there may also be 'procedural limitations' on the exercise of a power.

These limitations relate to the need for the decision maker to comply with statutory procedural requirements (for example, to give 'public notice' or 'reasons' or to advise a member of the public as to the existence of some right of appeal).

The courts developed the following rules for determining the legal consequences of a failure to comply with such requirements:

- The requirement was classified as either 'mandatory' or 'directory' in tenor.

Determining whether a particular requirement was mandatory or directory is never a simple task. The question was *not* simply whether the particular provision was mandatory or directory in its terms: see *Tasker v Fullwood* (1978).

The task of construction was to determine whether, having regard to the scope and object of the particular provision (and, indeed, of the whole statute or instrument), the legislature intended that a failure to comply with the stipulated requirement would invalidate the act done, or whether the validity of the act would be preserved notwithstanding non-compliance with the requirement: see *Tasker*.

- Where the procedural requirement was so called 'mandatory', it had to be strictly followed, otherwise the action taken would be void (or at least susceptible to being quashed by the court): see *Scurr v Brisbane City Council* (1973); *Haynes v Sutherland Shire Council* (1966); *Monaro Acclimatisation Society Inc v Minister for Planning* (1989).

Case examples

A retail trading company applied to the local council for development consent to the erection of a large discount department store. The relevant legislation required the council to cause the application to be advertised, with the advertisement to set out, among other things, 'particulars' of the application. The council's advertisement stated, in effect, that an application had been received for the erection of a single storey shop on a specified allotment of land. The advertisement did not specify the precise site of the proposed development or the area of land it would occupy. The High Court of Australia held that there had been non-compliance with the particular statutory requirement as to the giving of notice, which was held to be mandatory in nature and effect, and a condition precedent to any consideration of the application by the council. The court stated that the statutory provision was 'wholly dependent' upon the giving of public notice for the attainment of its objects.

Scurr v Brisbane City Council (1973)

An ordinance under the Local Government Act 1919 (NSW) stated that a local council had to call for tenders before entering into certain types of contracts. The specified procedure involved, among other things, the placing of one or more advertisements in a newspaper. The court held that the provisions were mandatory so as to affect validity.

Haynes v Sutherland Shire Council (1966)

- Breach of a so called 'directory' requirement would not ordinarily result in the action taken being void, provided there had been substantial compliance with the requirement: see *Ballina Environment Society Inc v Ballina Shire Council* (1992). (However, in some cases, even total non-compliance with the requirement would not affect the validity of what has been done: see *Victoria v Commonwealth* (1975); *London & Clydeside Estates Ltd v Aberdeen District Council* (1979).)

Case example

> A person had a statutory right to make a submission, by way of objection, to certain types of proposed developments. The relevant legislation required that any person seeking to make such a submission had to set forth in the submission the grounds of objection. The submission also had to be received by the consent authority within a certain time period. A local environmental group decided to make a submission, by way of objection, to a particular development. Due to shortness of time, the actual grounds of objection were not received within the stipulated time period, although the submission itself was. The court held that the statutory requirement as to the grounds of objection being set forth in the submission was directory only, in respect of which substantial compliance would suffice.

Ballina Environment Society Inc v Ballina Shire Council (1992)

Generally speaking, where:

- the impact of the action taken on private rights would be material; or
- the procedural requirement can be seen to be intended to assist the citizen in enforcing his or her rights,

then it was likely to be regarded as mandatory so as to affect validity. Examples of procedural requirements which had been held by the courts to be mandatory so as to affect validity include:

- Failure to give notice of a right of appeal within a specified period: see *London & Clydeside.*
- Failure to comply with advertising requirements in relation to tenders: see *Haynes v Sutherland Shire Council* (1966).
- Failure to comply with advertising requirements in relation to development proposals: see *Scurr v Brisbane City Council* (1973); *CSR Ltd t/as Readimix Group v Yarrowlumla Shire Council* (1985).

- Failure to prepare, submit or properly exhibit an environmental study, environmental impact statement or other document required by the relevant legislation: see *Prineas v Forestry Commission of New South Wales* (1983); *Monaro Acclimatisation Society Inc v Minister for Planning* (1989); *Penrith City Council v Waste Management Authority* (1990); *Gemsted Pty Ltd v Gosford City Council* (1993); *Curac v Shoalhaven City Council* (1993); *Byron Shire Businesses for the Future Inc v Byron Council* (the *Club Med* case) (1994); *Helman v Byron Shire Council* (1995).

- Failure to notify persons affected by proposed administrative orders in due time: see *Lee v Department of Education and Science* (1967).

More recently, in *Project Blue Sky Inc v Australian Broadcasting Authority* (1998), the High Court of Australia has held that the traditional test for determining whether the exercise of a statutory power was valid, by determining whether the legislative provision was 'mandatory' or 'directory', should not be used as it may focus attention on the wrong factors. Instead, a better test for determining the validity of the exercise of a statutory power is to ask whether it was a purpose of the legislation that an act done in breach of the provision should be invalid.

To put it another way, as Bignold J in *Ballina Environment Society Inc v Ballina Shire Council* (1992) inquired: '... can the purpose of the statutory requirement only be achieved by invalidating the result of any departure from it ... ?' In other words, having regard to the perceived statutory object of the provision in the overall scheme of the statute, what did the legislature intend to be the legal effect of non-compliance?

Extended *ultra vires*

Abuse of power

A donee of a statutory power must exercise that power strictly for the purpose for which it has been given, ultimately by the legislature: see *Warringah Shire Council v Pittwater Provisional Council* (1992).

Bad faith and improper purpose

A decision maker must not exercise its powers in bad faith or for an improper purpose: see *Sydney Municipal Council v Campbell* (1925);

Thompson v Randwick Municipal Council (1950); *Congreve v Home Office* (1976); *Re Toohey ex p Northern Land Council* (1981).

'Improper' in this context does not mean wrong or incorrect. It refers to something that is not a proper exercise of the power: see *Borkovic v Minister for Immigration and Ethnic Affairs* (1981). In other words, the power has been exercised for an ulterior purpose, that is, for a purpose other than the purpose for which the power was conferred: see *Thompson v Randwick Municipal Council* (1950).

Ultra vires

Simple/narrow *ultra vires*

- *Substantive*
  (including implied *ultra vires*)

- *Procedural*

Extended/broad *ultra vires*

- *Abuse of power:*
  - Bad faith
  - Improper purpose
  - Irrelevant considerations
  - Manifest unreasonableness
  - Lack of proportionality
  - Uncertainty (and lack of finality)
  - No evidence

- *Failure to exercise power:*
  - Fettering discretion
  - Acting on a policy
  - Acting under dictation
  - Sub-delegation
  - Estoppel

Although one must act in good faith in order to act honestly, bad faith is not necessarily the same thing as dishonesty.

Bad faith implies improper purpose.

Thompson v Randwick Municipal Council (1950)

The word 'honesty' (from the Latin, *honestas*, 'oneness') means *oneness with the truth, the facts.*

Case examples

A council sought to resume more land than was actually required for a town improvement scheme so that the surplus land could then be sold at a profit which would help defray the costs of the scheme. The court held that the council was not acting in good faith in that it had exercised its powers of compulsory acquisition for an ulterior purpose.

Thompson v Randwick Municipal Council (1950)

A minister who had a statutory power to revoke television licences exercised that power to revoke licences purchased early to avoid an increase in licence fees. The court held that the minister had used the power for an improper purpose; the power had been conferred to, for example, enable the minister to revoke licences obtained illegally, but the licences in question had not been obtained illegally.

Congreve v Home Office (1976)

Bad faith has clearly been recognised as a ground of challenge for abuse of power: see *Anisminic Ltd v Foreign Compensation Commission* (1969). However:

- It is difficult to find examples where it stands alone as the ground for attacking an administrative decision.
- It is usually an additional line of argument in cases where reliance is being placed on the fact that the decision in question is unreasonable or that irrelevant considerations have been taken into account: see below; see *Webb v Minister of Housing and Local Government* (1965). In fact, most exercises of a power in bad faith ordinarily would also be covered by those grounds of review.
- It is a much stronger claim than improper purpose and is more difficult to prove: see *Westminster Corporation v London & North Western Railway Co* (1905).

In the absence of malice, the making, without knowledge of its invalidity, of a decision which is devoid of legal effect is not conduct that of itself is capable of amounting to bad faith: see *Dunlop v Woollahra Municipal Council (No 2)* (1981).

However, the opposite of bad faith – good faith – calls for more than 'honest ineptitude': see *Mid Density Developments Pty Ltd v Rockdale Municipal Council* (1993).

Irrelevant considerations

A decision maker:

- must not base a decision on irrelevant or extraneous considerations; and

- must give due and proper consideration to all relevant considerations: see *Roberts v Hopwood* (1925); *Prescott v Birmingham Corporation* (1955); *Woolworths Properties Ltd v Ku-ring-gai Municipal Council* (1964); *Padfield v Minister of Agriculture, Fisheries and Food* (1968); *Bromley London Borough Council v Greater London Council* (1983); *R v ILEA ex p Westminster Council* (1986); *Parramatta City Council v Hale* (1982).

Case examples

> A council, which had statutory power to operate a public transport system and to charge such fares as it thought fit, decided to introduce free bus travel for old age pensioners. The court held that, although the council had the power to charge differential fares (and thus to grant concessions), the discretionary power still had to be exercised in accordance with ordinary business principles (a relevant consideration).
>
> *Prescott v Birmingham Corporation* (1955)

> A minister who was empowered to refer a complaint concerning milk prices fixed by a board under a milk marketing scheme to a committee of investigation refused to do so on the ground that if the committee upheld the complaint he would be expected to give effect to the committee's recommendation. The court held that the minister's fear of political embarrassment was an irrelevant consideration, as he was under a duty to act whenever there was a genuine complaint that the board was acting in a manner contrary to the public interest.
>
> *Padfield v Minister of Agriculture, Fisheries and Food* (1968)

The rules in relation to relevant and irrelevant considerations are as follows:

- The determination of what considerations are relevant and irrelevant is a matter of statutory construction.

- The statute may structure the decision maker's discretion by expressly enumerating the considerations to be taken into account. Where the statute does not do that, or the reviewing court decides that the enumerated factors are not exhaustive but merely inclusive, it will turn to the common law principles for ascertaining whether the power has been abused: see *Smith v Wyong Shire*

Council (1970); *Minister for Aboriginal Affairs v Peko-Wallsend Ltd* (1986).

- The relevant factors which a decision maker is bound to consider, and the irrelevant factors which it is bound not to consider, are then determined by implication from the subject matter, scope and purpose of the statute: see *Murphyores Inc Pty Ltd v Commonwealth* (1976); *Minister for Aboriginal Affairs v Peko-Wallsend Ltd* (1986).

- A general discretion, confined only by the scope and purposes of the legislation, will ordinarily be implied if the context, including the subject matter to be decided, provides no positive indication of the considerations by reference to which a decision is to be made: see *O'Sullivan v Farrer* (1989).

- The requirement to take into account all relevant considerations extends only to those considerations which the decision maker is bound, as opposed to entitled, to take into account: see *Minister for Aboriginal Affairs v Peko-Wallsend Ltd* (1986).

- A consideration which the decision maker is bound, as opposed to entitled, to take into account might nevertheless be so insignificant that the failure to take it into account could not have materially affected the decision: see *Minister for Aboriginal Affairs v Peko-Wallsend Ltd* (1986).

- Where a decision is reached on the basis of both relevant and irrelevant considerations, the court may decide which was the 'dominant' consideration. If it was an irrelevant consideration, the decision will be *ultra vires*: see *R v ILEA ex p Westminster Council* (1986). (This approach is more commonly used by the English courts.)

  Alternatively, and more commonly, at least in Australia, the court may apply the 'but for' test: see *Thompson v Randwick Municipal Council* (1950); *Samrein Pty Ltd v Metropolitan Water Sewerage and Drainage Board* (1982). In other words, would the decision maker still have reached the decision that it did 'but for' the irrelevant consideration?

- Generally speaking, the 'weight' to be given to each of the relevant heads of consideration is a matter for the decision maker, so long as all relevant matters are properly considered: see *Marnal Pty Ltd v Cessnock City Council* (1989).

- In some (rather rare) circumstances, however, the court may still set aside a decision on the ground that the decision is 'manifestly unreasonable': see *Associated Provincial Picture Houses Ltd v Wednesbury Corporation* (1948) where the decision maker:

) failed to give adequate weight to a relevant factor of great importance; or

) gave too much weight to a relevant factor of no great importance.

See *Minister for Aboriginal Affairs v Peko-Wallsend Ltd* (1986).

• A relevant consideration should not be considered in isolation from other relevant considerations: see *Geoffrey Twibill & Associates v Warringah Shire Council (No 3)* (1985).

A requirement to 'consider' some matter ordinarily denotes an obligation to give 'proper, genuine and realistic consideration' (to use the oft-quoted *dictum* of Gummow J in *Khan v Minister for Immigration and Ethnic Affairs* (1987)) to the matter.

Case example

> A local council granted development consent for the construction of a sports stadium in a public park. It was alleged that the council had failed to take into account certain relevant considerations. The court held that the council had not given the consideration which the relevant legislation directed it to give to such specified matters as parking, traffic and access. It was found that the councillors charged with the making of the decision had not had a proper opportunity to make an informed decision and did not have adequate information before them when they made their purported decision.
>
> *Parramatta City Council v Hale* (1982)

Manifest unreasonableness

A decision maker must not exercise its powers 'unreasonably' (in the sense that no reasonable decision maker, acting within the 'four corners of its jurisdiction', could ever have reached the decision in question): see *Associated Provincial Picture Houses Ltd v Wednesbury Corporation* (1948); *Parramatta City Council v Pestell* (1972); *Wheeler v Leicester County Council* (1985); *Prasad v Minister for Immigration and Ethnic Affairs* (1985); *Legal & General Life of Australia Ltd v North Sydney Municipal Council* (1989).

Case example

> A council, which was empowered to grant licences for cinemas subject to such conditions as it thought fit to impose, granted a licence to the cinema company subject to a condition that no children under the age of 15 years were to be admitted to any entertainment whether accompanied by an adult or not. The English Court of Appeal upheld the condition, saying that it was not a matter of what the court considered unreasonable.
>
> *Associated Provincial Picture Houses Ltd*
> *v Wednesbury Corporation* (1948)

Lord Greene MR in the *Wednesbury* case stated:

> The court is entitled to investigate the action of the local authority with a view to seeing whether they have taken into account matters which they ought not to have taken into account, or, conversely, have refused to take into account or neglected to take into account matters which they ought to take into account. Once that question is answered in favour of the local authority, it may be still possible to say that, although the local authority have kept within the four corners of the matters which they ought to consider, they have nevertheless come to a conclusion *so unreasonable that no reasonable authority could ever have come to it*. [Emphasis added.]

Where *Wednesbury* unreasonableness is alleged with respect to a decision of councillors in, for example, a town planning matter, the burden is on the challenger to demonstrate, in effect, a decision 'verging on an absurdity': see *Legal & General Life of Australia Ltd v North Sydney Municipal Council* (1989).

Lack of proportionality

A decision may be so lacking in reasonable proportionality as 'not to be a real exercise of the power': see *South Australia v Tanner* (1989).

Although lack of proportionality as a ground of review has yet to receive full judicial acceptance in Australia, particularly in the context of general administrative decision making (as opposed to subordinate legislation), there have been suggestions that the principle may have an application beyond subordinate legislation: see *State of New South Wales v Macquarie Bank Ltd* (1992). See also *Koh v South Australia* (1989).

Even in England, the House of Lords has taken the view that proportionality is but part of *Wednesbury* unreasonableness: see *R v Home Office ex p Brind* (1991).

In *Australian Broadcasting Tribunal v Bond* (1990), Deane J suggested a minimum standard of proportionality in the judicial or quasi-judicial actions of a statutory tribunal.

Uncertainty (and lack of finality)
A decision maker must make decisions which are 'certain' and 'final'. In that regard, a decision may be declared invalid if:

- the exercise of the power leads to a result that is so uncertain that no reasonable person could comply with it: see *Television Corporation Ltd v Commonwealth* (1963); or
- it cannot be given any sensible meaning (but not merely because it is ambiguous or could lead to uncertain results): see *Fawcett Properties Ltd v Buckingham County Council* (1961).

Certain types of administrative decisions, such as an approval or a consent granted by a local council, the making of which is intended to finalise the issues raised by the subject application for the approval or consent, must possess 'finality': see *Randwick Municipal Council v Pacific-Seven Pty Ltd* (1989).

No evidence
See Chapter 3.

Failure to exercise power

Note: Some commentators use the compendious expression 'retention of discretion' to describe the need for a decision maker to retain a discretion in the exercise of a power. Fettering discretion, acting inflexibly on a policy, acting under dictation, and unauthorised sub-delegation offend against the 'retention of discretion' rule. In more traditional terms, the commission of any one or more of those acts results in a 'constructive' failure to exercise power, leaving the discretionary power constructively unexercised.

Fettering discretion
A decision maker must not fetter itself in advance as to how it will exercise its statutory discretion, whether by way of contract, estoppel or otherwise: see *Wilkinson v Tamarang Shire Council* (1932); *NSW Trotting Club Ltd v Glebe Municipal Council* (1937); *Ransom & Luck Ltd v Surbiton Borough Council* (1949); *South Australia v Commonwealth* (1962); *Lower Hutt County Council v Banks* (1974); *Doran Developments Pty Ltd v*

Newcastle City Council (1984); *Steeples v Derbyshire County Council* (1984).

This means that a decision maker, entrusted with a discretionary power:

- Cannot act in a manner which purports to divest itself of its ability to perform its functions in the future.

    However, not all divesting is unlawful. Some acts of so called divesting (for example, contracts, delegations) have been upheld as not being against the public interest: see *British Transport Commission v Westmorland County Council* (1958); *Sutton v Warringah Shire Council* (1987).

- Cannot bind itself to exercise a function in a particular manner.

    Thus, it is not appropriate for, say, a local council to make an agreement with a developer whereby the council agrees, for instance, to do everything in its power to obtain the necessary consent for the particular development to proceed. In addition, the council must ensure that its position as a planning and consent authority is not compromised by its position as, for example, landowner or lessor: see *Anderton v Auckland City Council* (1978).

    If an agreement could have a 'material and significant effect' on the decision maker's decision, the decision will be voidable or void: see *Steeples v Derbyshire County Council* (1984).

Case example

A local council had entered into an agreement to lease certain land to a developer for a leisure park with extensive facilities. The development required development consent from the council. The council, in its agreement with the developer, bound itself to take all reasonable steps to obtain the necessary grant of consent. The agreement went on to provide that in the event that the council failed to use its best endeavours to obtain consent, it was liable to pay a substantial sum of money by way of liquidated damages. In due course the council granted development consent to the proposed development. The court stated that fettering of discretion would occur if a reasonable person would regard such an agreement as being likely to have a 'material and significant' effect one way or another on the outcome of the decision in question. The court went on to say that it may very well be that something appearing to have 'less of an effect than that' might also constitute a fettering of discretion.

Steeples v Derbyshire County Council (1984)

However, once again, not every agreement by which a decision maker purports to restrict its discretion is necessarily *ultra vires*. The question is whether it is contrary to the public interest. There may be cases where the advantages gained by the decision maker as a *quid pro quo* for the restriction are in the public interest and outweigh any public detriment that may flow from the restriction accepted by the decision maker: see *Bruce Kerr Pty Ltd v Gosford City Council* (1978).

- Must also act impartially and must not prejudge the issues in a particular matter: see *R v Glenelg Town ex p Pier House Pty Ltd* (1968).

The holding of provisional or preformed views on a matter will not, in itself, constitute predetermination.

The decision maker's mind must not be so foreclosed that it gives no genuine consideration to the matter in question: see *Franklin v Minister of Town and Country Planning* (1948); *R v Amber Valley District Council ex p Jackson* (1984).

Acting on a policy

A decision maker:

- must examine in detail each matter before it on its merits; and
- must not automatically (or inflexibly) apply an overall policy without considering the particular circumstances of the matter before it: see *R v Port of London Authority ex p Kynoch Ltd* (1919); *British Oxygen Co Ltd v Minister of Technology* (1971); *Emmott v Ku-ring-gai Municipal Council* (1954); *BOMA v Sydney City Council* (1984).

Thus, a local council cannot categorically take the position that all lots of a certain shape (for example, 'battle-axe' lots) will not receive subdivision approval: see *Emmott v Ku-ring-gai Municipal Council* (1954).

A decision maker does not, however, act unlawfully in adopting policies to structure its discretionary powers: see *R v Eastleigh Borough Council ex p Betts* (1983).

Indeed, the application of a stated policy to decision making ensures consistency and fairness: see *Re Drake v Minister for Immigration and Ethnic Affairs (No 2)* (1979).

Where a decision maker has adopted a policy in relation to the exercise of a discretionary power:

- The policy must not conflict with the relevant statute or be so rigid that it cannot be departed from in appropriate cases: see *Re Becker and Minister for Immigration and Ethnic Affairs* (1977).
- Each matter must still be considered on its merits.
- Even if the policy 'leans against' granting approval to the type of application in question:
  - ○ the decision maker must not refuse 'to listen to anyone with something new to say': see *British Oxygen Co Ltd v Minister of Technology* (1971); and
  - ○ an opportunity must always be given to the applicant to show cause why the policy ought not to apply, or ought to apply with certain modifications, in his or her particular case.

A policy is not unlawful merely because it:

- excludes consideration of some relevant factors; or
- attributes great weight to certain specified factors: see *Re Findlay* (1985).

Provided any other relevant factors are taken into account in the course of deciding whether an individual case is so exceptional it escapes the normal application of the policy, such an application of policy is not *ultra vires*: see also *R v Torquay Licensing JJ ex p Brockman* (1951).

Finally, where numerous applications of a similar kind have to be considered and determined (and, presumably, there will be no deprivation of individual rights), a more automatic application of a policy is permissible: *British Oxygen Co Ltd v Minister of Technology* (1971); *Peninsula Anglican Boys' School v Ryan* (1985). However, the decision maker is still obliged to consider any 'special pleading'.

Acting under dictation

A decision maker, entrusted with a statutory discretion:

- must exercise that power itself and in an independent manner; and
- must not be dictated to by a third party: see *R v Stepney Corporation* (1902); *Evans v Donaldson* (1909).

'Dictation' occurs where the decision maker feels obliged to decide a matter in a particular way because of another's conclusions in relation to the matter, even if the third party:

- does not intend to dictate (*Stepney*); or

- has given no direction that a particular approach should be followed (*Evans*).

Case example

> A council, having abolished the office of vestry clerk, was required by statute to pay compensation to the holder of the abolished office. For that purpose, the statute provided that, in fixing the quantum of compensation, the council was required to consider various specified matters. The council's town clerk wrote to the Treasury and obtained its formula for calculating compensation in similar cases. The court held that, in using the Treasury's formula, the council had failed to exercise its own statutory discretion and to consider the person's particular case.

> *R v Stepney Corporation* (1902)

There are, however, certain qualifications to the rule against dictation:

- A decision maker such as a local government authority is entitled to have regard to the views of a statutory body or government department whose functions impinge upon a council domain, although it is not strictly bound by those views: see *Wiggins v Kogarah Municipal Council* (1958); *Tracey v Waverley Municipal Council* (1959); *Amoco Aust Pty Ltd v Albury City Council* (1965).
- The rule may not apply with the same stringency – and may not even apply at all – in the context of government departmental decision making (at least at a high level): see *R v Anderson ex p Ipec-Air Pty Ltd* (1965); *Ansett Transport Industries (Operations) Pty Ltd v Commonwealth* (1977). Where a discretionary power is given to a public servant, there may be a right or even a duty to accept policy directions from ministers.

Sub-delegation

A decision maker, entrusted with the making of a decision, cannot delegate the making of the decision to some other person or body.

This rule is always subject to express provision to the contrary: see ss 744 and 745 of the Local Government Act 1993 (NSW).

Estoppel

Estoppel, as such, is not a separate ground of extended *ultra vires*, but may militate against other such grounds (for example, fettering discretion).

As mentioned above, it is a general principle of administrative law that a decision maker cannot fetter itself in advance as to how it will perform its statutory duty or exercise its statutory discretion, whether by way of contract, estoppel or otherwise.

Until fairly recent times:

- The courts generally were most reluctant to invoke estoppel in the context of a statutory framework: see *Rocca v Ryde Municipal Council* (1961); *Southend-on-Sea Corporation v Hodgson (Wickford) Ltd* (1962); *Wormald v Gioia* (1980); *Western Fish Products Ltd v Penrith District Council* (1981).

- Estoppel could, however, operate where the decision maker made a representation (as to some state of affairs or the terms of the proposed decision) of fact, but not of law: see *Wormald v Gioia* (1980); *Brickworks Ltd v Warringah Shire Council* (1963).

- Estoppel would not operate where the relevant representation or other administrative action was *ultra vires*, because that would be to violate another administrative law principle (namely, the doctrine of *ultra vires*): see *Maritime Electric Co Ltd v General Dairies Ltd* (1937); *Howell v Falmouth Boat Construction Co Ltd* (1951).

- There were, however, two exceptions to the principle that estoppel could not operate in relation to *ultra vires* actions: see *Western Fish Products Ltd v Penrith District Council* (1981):
  - ◦ where the officer had actual delegated authority or ostensible authority to make the representation or take the action in question;
  - ◦ where the administrative decision maker had a regular practice of waiving a procedural requirement of the kind in question.

Since the High Court's decision in *Walton's Stores (Interstate) Ltd v Maher* (1988), there have been several cases in which estoppel has been held to operate in the context of administrative decision making, even in relation to *ultra vires* actions: see, for example, *Waverley Transit Pty Ltd v Metropolitan Transit Authority* (1988); *Kurtovic v Minister for Immigration, Local Government and Ethnic Affairs* (1989); *Rubrico v Minister for Immigration, Local Government and Ethnic Affairs* (1989); *Vanden Pty Ltd v Blue Mountains City Council* (1992).

It would now appear that the reviewing court will approach the matter on the basis of whether the conduct of the decision maker was 'unconscionable'. The party seeking relief would need to show that it would be unjust or otherwise inequitable to allow the decision maker to resile from its promise, undertaking, assurance or conduct.

Case example

A statutory authority was responsible for regulating metropolitan bus services. Having encouraged an existing bus operator in the belief that its contract would be renewed, the authority then proceeded to accept the tender of another operator. The court found that the authority had acted unconscionably and restrained it from proceeding with the agreement with the other operator.

Waverley Transit Pty Ltd v Metropolitan Transit Authority (1988)

5 Jurisdictional Error

You should be familiar with the following areas:

- the distinction between traditional jurisdictional error and broad or extended jurisdictional error
- the three different types of traditional jurisdictional error
- the concept of a 'constructive' jurisdictional error
- the jurisdictional fact doctrine
- the fact/law distinction
- the concept of error of law on the face of the record
- the different types of privative clauses and their efficacy or otherwise

Introduction

The doctrine of jurisdictional error:

- in its modern form can be traced from the 17th century when it came to be used to control the activities of inferior courts and quasi-judicial statutory tribunals; and
- is very similar to the doctrine of *ultra vires* which became a means of ensuring that executive and administrative authorities (including local government authorities) acted within their powers. One doctrine speaks in terms of 'jurisdiction', the other in terms of 'power'.

In recent years, the doctrines of jurisdictional error and *ultra vires* have become very closely associated and in England the distinction between them has, for all practical purposes, been obliterated as a result of the House of Lords' decision in *Anisminic Ltd v Foreign Compensation Commission* (1969).

In Australia, for the most part, the distinction between the two doctrines remains, reflecting different approaches by the courts to the question of whether or not to intervene by way of judicial review.

Ultra vires and jurisdictional error

	Ultra vires	Jurisdictional error
History	*Mid-19th century* Railway companies, independent statutory bodies, etc	*17th century* Inferior courts, statutory tribunals
Powers	Administrative, subordinate legislation	Judicial, quasi-judicial
Remedies	Mandamus Injunction Declaration	Prohibition Certiorari

---

Relief in the nature of certiorari (see Chapter 6) is commonly used to deal with jurisdictional errors and so called errors of law 'on the face of the record' (see below).

Errors of law and errors of fact

In judicial review proceedings, the distinction between questions (and errors) of fact and questions (and errors) of law is critical.

The so called 'fact/law distinction' is quite complex and a full analysis of the topic is beyond the scope of this book.

Questions of fact

Questions of fact include:

- Questions on which reasonable persons might reasonably arrive at divergent conclusions: see *Federal Commissioner of Taxation v Miller* (1946).
- Questions in respect of which the reviewing court would find it very difficult to form an independent opinion without hearing all the evidence.
- The 'ordinary' meaning of a statutory word or phrase: see *NSW Associated Blue-Metal Quarries Ltd v Federal Commissioner of Taxation* (1956).
- Perverse or wrong findings of fact, findings of fact contrary to the weight of or against the evidence, and unsound reasoning: see *Azzopardi v Tasman UEB Industries Ltd* (1985).
- Whether evidence ought to be accepted: see *Azzopardi*.

Facts

1   Logic is about *things*, not thought, and how things are related. Sound (logical) thinking means relating (that is, putting together or distinguishing) different pieces of information about facts or alleged facts. We do not merely think. We always think *of* situations and events. It is *always* a case of ... what is.

2   There is only *one* way or level of being ('reality'), that of *occurrence*, that is, ordinary things occurring in space and time. A single logic applies to all things and how they are related.

3   A fact is an occurrence in space and time, a 'thing in itself' – in other words ... what *is*! Reality! Its occurrence or existence is not dependent or constituted by being known. Nothing is constituted by, nor can it be defined or explained by reference to, the relations it has to other things.

For example, any administrative decision making process is a 'relation' involving:

• the person who decides a particular matter (that is, the administrative decision maker),

• the act of deciding the matter (that is, the administrative decision making process), and

• the matter decided (that is, the administrative decision),

– three separate things, none of which, in logic, is 'constituted' by its relations to any of the others, nor 'dependent' on any of the others.

Further, if I specify something only by the relations it has to myself or other things (for example, person X *is* 'unfit' to continue to be registered as an employer because I *consider* person X to be 'unfit' or because person X has acted in the manner Y), we know *nothing* about the thing itself (that is, whether person X *is* 'unfit', and what *is* an unfit person). The *fact* that I *consider* some person to be 'unfit' does not logically imply anything intrinsic to that thing itself (the *ultimate* question of fact). To use the *fact* of a person being *considered* to be 'unfit' as a determinant or an indication of the person *being* 'unfit' (an objective character of things), independent information is needed about the sorts of things that enter into the particular relation (that is, information as to the characteristics of 'unfit' persons and their presence or absence in the person concerned). See *R v Australian Stevedoring Industry Board ex p Melbourne Stevedoring Co Pty Ltd* (1953) in which, although a subjective test of 'unfitness' was contained in the relevant legislation (that is, one's being 'satisfied' that a particular person was 'unfit'), the court, after considering what the word 'unfitness' connoted, was still able to hold on the facts of the particular case that there were no objective grounds for saying that the particular employer was 'unfit'.

4   The logical form of any statement or proposition (including any belief, value, opinion, idea or ideal) will reveal it to be asserting some matter of *fact*, whether truly or falsely. A question of fact always arises and, no matter how complex, is decidable and verifiable or falsifiable, once the necessary criteria have been laid

down. It is a plain matter of fact whether those criteria are satisfied in a particular case. That is true even with respect to opinions.

5   Ideas or opinions can be said to be true or false when attention is directed, *not* to the idea or opinion itself, but to the thing that the idea or opinion is *of*. The test of a true idea or opinion is to see whether or not something *is* the case.

6   To find out whether a fact exists, you 'look and see' or observe. (NOTE: Observation is not necessarily restricted to sense-perception.)

7   A fact can be explained *only* as following logically from other facts on the same level of observability. For example, whether or not there is a 'furnished dwelling-house' (an 'ultimate' question of fact) involves the following questions of 'primary fact', all of which are logically interconnected on the same order or level of being:

- Is there a 'structure' (that is, something built up of component parts)?

- If so, is there a structure in the nature of a 'building' (a question of fact and degree in each particular case)?

- If so, does the building comprise a 'dwelling' (that is, a room or suite of rooms occupied or used or so constructed or adapted as to be capable of being occupied or used as a separate domicile)?

- If so, is the dwelling 'furnished'?

Questions of law

Questions of law include:

- Questions in respect of which the reviewing court is of the opinion that it is more equipped to decide: see *ex p Wurth; Re Tully* (1954).

- The sense (legal or otherwise) in which a statute uses a word or phrase: see *NSW Associated Blue-Metal Quarries* (1956).

- The 'legal' meaning of a statutory word or phrase: see *Australian Gas Light Company v Valuer General* (1940).

- Whether there is evidence of a particular fact, and whether the evidence reasonably admits of different conclusions: see *Azzopardi* (1985); *Federal Commissioner of Taxation v Broken Hill South Ltd* (1941).

- Whether inferences and conclusions as to primary facts can reasonably be drawn: see *Australian Gas Light Company* (1940); *Edwards v Bairstow* (1956).

- Whether primary facts, fully found, are capable of falling within the ambit of a statutory description: see *Federal Commissioner of Taxation v Miller* (1946). (Whether those facts actually so fall is ordinarily a question of fact and there will *only* be an error of law where *only one* conclusion can be drawn as to whether the facts fall within a statutory description and a contrary conclusion has been drawn by the original decision maker: see *Hope v Bathurst City Council* (1980); *Londish v Knox Grammar School* (1997).)

- Misdirection in law, misconstruction of the statute, application of the wrong legal test, and defining otherwise than in accordance with law the question of fact to be answered (at least with respect to 'ultimate', if not primary, findings of fact): see *Azzopardi*.

The courts, generally speaking, reserve the final say in the matter where the critical issue is a question of:

- the interpretation of the statutory language; or
- the source of the relevant power.

Case example

> Calls paid on shares in a company carrying on 'mining operations' could be claimed by a taxpayer as deductions from assessable income under income tax legislation. A board of review had concluded that a particular company was engaged in 'mining operations'. That decision was made the subject of a statutory right of appeal on a question of law to the High Court of Australia. Different approaches were taken by the various judges to distinguishing between questions of fact and questions of law. Rich ACJ was of the view that the question whether the material facts, fully found, fell within the ambit of the statutory description, was one of law. Starke and Williams JJ were of the opinion that, whilst the word 'mining operations' was not a term of art and its meaning was a question of fact, the question whether on the evidence the review board could have reasonably concluded that the company was engaged in the carrying on of 'mining operations' was a question of law. McTiernan J was of the view that the question was one of fact, being one which the members of the review board were 'peculiarly fitted to decide'.
>
> *Federal Commissioner of Taxation v Broken Hill South Ltd* (1941)

Errors in fact-finding

As to errors in fact-finding, the general common law principles are as follows:

- An error in fact-finding does not necessarily constitute an error of law.

  For the most part, the reviewing court is slow to interfere with erroneous findings, inferences and conclusions of fact, particularly where the question is:

  - ⊃ one on which reasonable persons might reasonably arrive at divergent conclusions: see Bendles Motors Ltd v Bristol Corporation (1963); Azzopardi v Tasman UEB Industries Ltd (1985);

  - ⊃ a matter of opinion, policy or taste.

- Merely making a wrong finding of fact or demonstrating unsound reasoning is not, in itself, an error of law: see *Azzopardi*.

- The making of a finding, or the drawing of an inference, in the absence of evidence or supporting probative material is, however, an error of law.

- Failure to take into account a relevant consideration is not an error of law where the fact-finding does not involve the exercise of a discretion (that is, where the decision maker is obliged to act in a particular way if a certain state of affairs exists or appears to exist): see *Minister for Immigration and Ethnic Affairs v Teo* (1995).

The legal position is somewhat different under the Administrative Decisions (Judicial Review) Act 1977 (Cth): see Chapter 8.

Traditional jurisdictional error

Errors of law (as opposed to errors of fact) may be classified according to whether or not they go to jurisdiction.

The commission of a jurisdictional error results in a *void* decision, whereas the commission of a non-jurisdictional error of law only results in a *voidable* decision.

A jurisdictional error, in traditional terms, is of three kinds:

1 A *want* (or *lack*) of jurisdiction: that is, there is an absence of power or authority on the part of the decision maker to make the decision (cf substantive *ultra vires*).

Case example

A board, which had jurisdiction to settle disputes between employers and employees in the coal mining industry, decided that a firm of haulage contractors, some of whose lorry drivers carried coal, was engaged in the coal mining industry and therefore bound to comply with an industrial award applicable to lorry drivers in that industry. The High Court found that the drivers were employed as lorry drivers generally (also carrying firewood, timber, blue metal and other materials) and not as carriers of coal. The board's decision was made without jurisdiction.

R v Hickman ex p Fox and Clinton (1945)

2   An *excess* of jurisdiction: that is, the decision is within the general power or authority of the decision maker, but there is a lack of jurisdiction occurring somewhere throughout the decision making process itself (cf procedural *ultra vires*).

Case example

Regulations made provision for alteration of a rate of wages if an industrial authority was 'satisfied' that the rates of remuneration were 'anomalous' and the new award was approved by the responsible minister. An increased rate of wages was awarded to shift workers at certain collieries. The High Court found that, whilst some of the rates of wages may have been such that there were reasons for altering them, the existence of an 'anomaly' had not been established. The board's 'opinion' as to the existence of an anomaly was not correctly based on the law and therefore did not exist.

R v Connell ex p Hetton Bellbird Collieries Ltd (1944)

3   A wrongful *failure* or *refusal* to exercise jurisdiction: that is, there is no lack or excess of jurisdiction, but simply no exercise, or proper exercise, of it.

Case example

A mining warden, if 'of the opinion that the public interest or right [would] be prejudicially affected by the granting of an application for a mining lease', was obliged to recommend to the responsible minister that the application be rejected. The warden, after conducting an inquiry, decided to recommend to the minister that a company's application for mining leases be granted, stating that a certain objector represented only a 'section of the public'. The

High Court found that the warden had drawn an irrelevant distinction between the views of a section of the public and the public interest as a whole, thus confusing the person who made the submission with the nature and extent of the objection (which went to the public interest). The warden, in misconceiving his duty, failed to perform his duty.

Sinclair v Mining Warden at Maryborough (1975)

A non-jurisdictional error of law, in traditional terms, is any other error of law. In that regard, a superior court, in judicial review proceedings, draws a distinction between:

- matters which are *within* the original decision maker's jurisdiction (commonly referred to as matters 'going to the merits'), that is, those matters which the decision maker alone decides; and

- matters which are *outside* the original decision maker's jurisdiction (so called jurisdictional matters), that is, those matters which must be established as a condition precedent for the decision maker to exercise its jurisdiction.

Errors made with respect to:

- matters *within* jurisdiction – whether of fact or law – are unreviewable (in the absence of some statutory right of appeal) unless the original decision maker has made an error of law which is apparent 'on the face of the record' (see below);

- jurisdictional matters (including errors made with respect to so called 'jurisdictional facts') are reviewable for 'jurisdictional error'.

A jurisdictional fact is some fact which must exist as a condition precedent, or essential prerequisite, for the decision maker to exercise its jurisdiction.

Example

The legislature sets up a special statutory tribunal to determine the fair rent for a furnished dwelling-house. Whether a particular building is a dwelling-house, and whether it is furnished, are questions of jurisdictional fact, because those facts must be established as conditions precedent for the tribunal to exercise its jurisdiction. Thus, if the tribunal purports to determine the fair rent for, say, an unfurnished dwelling-house, a building other than a dwelling-house, or a structure other than a building, it will have made a jurisdictional error. However, the amount of rent determined for a furnished dwelling-house would, under the traditional doctrine of jurisdictional error, be a matter within jurisdiction and, thus, not amenable to judicial review.

Traditional jurisdictional error

1   Want/lack of jurisdiction
Absence of power or authority to make a decision

2   Excess of jurisdiction
Within general power or authority but lack of jurisdiction occurring throughout the decision making process

3   Wrongful failure/refusal to exercise jurisdiction
No lack or excess of jurisdiction
Jurisdiction, but no exercise of it

Error of law on the face of the record

Error of law on the face of the record is:

- a ground of review first developed in England in the 17th century;
- an exception to the traditional doctrine of jurisdictional error which states that only errors going to jurisdiction are reviewable by a superior court at common law.

Under this exception to the traditional doctrine, any error of law appearing on the face of the record of an inferior court or tribunal is reviewable, regardless of whether or not the error is jurisdictional.
The error must:

- be one of *law* (and not of fact); and
- appear *plainly* 'on the face of the record'.

At first, 'the record' was held to comprise only:

- the document or documents initiating the subject proceedings;
- the pleadings (if any); and
- the adjudication.

It did not include the evidence or the reasons for the decision (unless the tribunal actually chose to incorporate them): see *R v Northumberland Compensation Appeal Tribunal ex p Shaw* (1952).

The record later came to:

- include 'not only the formal order, but all those documents which appear therefrom to be the basis of the decision – that on which it is grounded': see *Baldwin & Francis Ltd v Patents Appeal Tribunal* (1959), *per* Lord Denning; and

- embrace, at least in England, the transcript of the proceedings (in particular, the reasons contained in the transcript).

Thus, in *R v Knightsbridge Crown Court ex p International Sporting Club (London) Ltd* (1982), the Divisional Court held that the reasons contained in the transcript of an oral judgment of a court were part of the record of that court, for the purpose of granting certiorari for error of law on the face of the record.

That view had been followed by various Australian superior courts, in particular, the NSW Court of Appeal: see *GJ Coles & Co Ltd v Retail Trade Industrial Tribunal and Others* (1987); *Commissioner of Motor Transport v Kirkpatrick* (1987); *Commissioner for Motor Transport v Kirkpatrick* (1988); *Commissioner of Police v District Court of New South Wales and Another* (1993).

However, the High Court in *Craig v South Australia* (1995) has:

- expressly rejected expansive formulations of the record for the purposes of certiorari;

- observed that there is no fixed rule as to what constitutes the record in a particular case; and

- concluded that the record at common law ordinarily does *not* include the transcript of the earlier proceedings, nor the reasons for the decision, unless they were actually incorporated in the tribunal's formal order or decision.

Under statute, the position may well be different: see, for example, s 69(4) of the Supreme Court Act 1970 (NSW).

Extended jurisdictional error

In England, the distinction between jurisdictional and non-jurisdictional errors of law has, for all intents and purposes, been abolished as a result of the House of Lords' decision in *Anisminic Ltd v Foreign Compensation Commission* (1969).

Case example

> The appellants were a British company which had owned a mining property in Egypt. The property had been sequestrated by the Egyptian government during the Suez crisis. A sum of money was subsequently made available by the Egyptian government for distribution by the British government at the latter's discretion. Determination of claims to that money was referred by statute to a special commission. The commission rejected the appellants' claim for compensation, on the ground that they had not satisfied the requirements of a statutory order in council. The order relevantly provided that a claim was to be treated as having been established if the applicant was a person named in a specified treaty as the owner of identified property or the successor in title of such a person, provided that the person so named *and* the successor in title were British nationals at specified dates. The commission held that, although the appellants were named in the treaty, the property in question had been sold to an Egyptian organisation (TEDO) which was not, therefore, a British national. Accordingly, the commission held that the appellants were not entitled under the order in council. The House of Lords held that the commission had made a jurisdictional error in misconstruing the phrase 'successor in title' and in taking an irrelevant consideration into account (viz the nationality of TEDO). Their Lordships held that the appellants, as the original owners of the subject property, did not have to prove that both they and any successor in title were British nationals. The commission was found to have made an inquiry which the order did not empower it to make and to have based its decision on a matter which it had no right to take into account.

> *Anisminic Ltd v Foreign Compensation Commission* (1969)

The effect of the majority's reasoning in that case was to extend the traditional concept of jurisdictional error to embrace errors of law not traditionally thought to go to jurisdiction, namely, errors of law of the kind subsumed within broad or extended *ultra vires*.

Lord Reid said:

> But there are many cases where, although the tribunal had jurisdiction to enter on the inquiry, it has done or failed to do something in the course of the inquiry which is of such a nature that its decision is a nullity. It may have given its decision in bad faith. It may have made a decision which it has no power to make.

It may have failed in the course of the inquiry to comply with the requirements of natural justice. It may in perfect good faith have misconstrued the provisions giving it power to act so that it failed to deal with the question remitted to it and decided some question which was not remitted to it. It may have refused to take into account something which it was required to take into account. Or it may have based its decision on some matter which, under the provisions setting it up, it had no right to take into account. I do not intend this list to be exhaustive.

Lord Pearce, preferring to use the single expression 'lack of jurisdiction' to embrace traditional jurisdictional errors as well as various errors of law not traditionally regarded as going to jurisdiction, said:

Lack of jurisdiction may arise in various ways. There may be an absence of those formalities or things which are conditions precedent to the tribunal having any jurisdiction to embark on an inquiry. Or the tribunal may at the end make an order that it has no jurisdiction to make. Or in the intervening stage, while engaged on a proper inquiry, the tribunal may depart from the rules of natural justice; or it may ask itself the wrong questions; or it may take into account matters which it was not directed to take into account. Thereby it would step outside its jurisdiction. It would turn its inquiry into something not directed by Parliament and fail to make the inquiry which Parliament did direct. Any of these things would cause its purported decision to be a nullity.

The House of Lords in *Anisminic* expressly recognised the continued existence of a distinction between reviewable errors of law going to jurisdiction and unreviewable errors on matters going to the merits, but took such a broad view of what matters went to jurisdiction that it soon became almost impossible to conceive of any error of law which would not, in the opinion of the majority Lords, go to jurisdiction.

The so called '*Anisminic* revolution' (HWR Wade) then unfolded over a 15 year period, as follows:

- Lord Diplock, in 1974, made an extra-judicial statement (see 'Administrative law: judicial review reviewed' (1974) 33 Camb LJ 233) to the effect that *Anisminic* had rendered obsolete the distinction between jurisdictional and non-jurisdictional errors of law.

- In 1981, the distinction between jurisdictional and non-jurisdictional errors of law was declared abolished, for all practical purposes, but only in respect of administrative tribunals (and not inferior courts): see *Re Racal Communications Ltd* (1981), *per* Lord Diplock.

- In 1983, Lord Diplock suggested that the distinction had also been abolished for inferior courts as well as administrative tribunals: see *O'Reilly v Mackman* (1983).
- By 1984, any restriction in relation to inferior courts, to the extent (if any) to which it still existed in England, had gone completely: see *R v Greater Manchester Coroner ex p Tal* (1984).

The result of the *Anisminic* decision, in jurisdictions where it is accepted, is that:

- The distinction between the two doctrines of *ultra vires* and jurisdictional error has, for all practical purposes, been obliterated.
- For all practical purposes, every error of law is, even in the absence of a statutory right of review or appeal, *prima facie* reviewable.
- The only important dichotomy is the distinction between error of law and error of fact.
- The concept of 'error of law on the face of the record' has been made redundant: see *R v Hull University Visitor ex p Page* (1992).

Example

Assume, once again, that the legislature has set up a special statutory tribunal to determine the fair rent for a furnished dwelling-house. The tribunal purports to determine a 'fair rent' of $2,000 per week for both furnished and unfurnished dwelling-houses. Under the *Anisminic* doctrine of extended jurisdictional error, the tribunal's purported determinations may be challenged on the ground of manifest unreasonableness (in that a rent of $2,000 might be argued to be excessive). In addition, the tribunal's purported determination in respect of unfurnished dwelling-houses could be challenged on the ground of improper purpose (in that the tribunal is purporting to regulate unfurnished property).

Ultra vires and jurisdictional error

Ultra vires	Jurisdictional error
Simple/Narrow:	**Traditional:**
Substantive *ultra vires*	Want/lack of jurisdiction
Procedural *ultra vires*	Excess of jurisdiction
	Wrongful failure (including a a 'constructive failure') or refusal to exercise jurisdiction
Extended/Broad:	**Extended:**
For example, bad faith, denial of procedural fairness, irrelevant considerations, unreasonableness	Errors of law corresponding with extended/broad *ultra vires*, as well as errors of law corresponding with simple/narrow *ultra vires*

Extended jurisdictional error in Australia

Most Australian superior courts continue to maintain a distinction between jurisdictional and non-jurisdictional errors of law: see *R v Industrial Commission of South Australia ex p Adelaide Milk Supply Co-operative Ltd (No 2)* (1978); *R v Ward ex p Bowering* (1978); *Darkingung*

Local Aboriginal Land Council v Minister for Natural Resources (No 2) (1987); *Public Service Association of South Australia v Federated Clerks' Union of Australia, South Australian Branch* (1991); *Carter v Drake* (1992); *Commissioner of Police v District Court of New South Wales* (1993); *Walker v Industrial Court of New South Wales* (1994); *Craig v South Australia* (1995); cf *Thelander v Woodward* (1981).

The High Court decision in *Craig* is the first occasion on which the court has displayed an almost unambiguous openness towards the *Anisminic* doctrine of extended jurisdictional error, *at least* as regards administrative tribunals.

It was said in *Craig* that if an administrative tribunal:

> falls into an error of law which causes it to identify a wrong issue, to ask itself a wrong question, to ignore relevant material, to rely on irrelevant material or, at least in some circumstances, to make an erroneous finding or to reach a mistaken conclusion, and the tribunal's exercise or purported exercise of power is thereby affected, it exceeds its authority or powers. Such an error of law is jurisdictional error which will invalidate any order or decision of the tribunal which reflects it.

Admittedly, the court's comments in relation to administrative tribunals – as opposed to inferior courts – are, strictly speaking, *obiter*. Be that as it may, the following conclusions may reasonably be drawn – albeit somewhat tentatively – from the court's decision:

1   The traditional distinction between jurisdictional errors of law on the one hand and non-jurisdictional errors of law on the other still exists, at least as regards inferior courts and analogous quasi-judicial statutory tribunals.

2   However, even as regards inferior courts and analogous tribunals, there is still the possibility that such a body *may* commit a reviewable jurisdictional error of the *Anisminic* type (for example, a failure to take into account some matter which ought to have been taken into account).

Ordinarily, that will not be the case. Much would appear to depend upon whether the error in question may be said to be one on which the decision of the case depends: see *Pearlman v Keepers and Governors of Harrow School* (1979). The answer to that question would appear to be one of degree on the facts of each particular case.

In *Edwards v Justice Giudice* (1999), Finkelstein J expressed the opinion that an error of law will relevantly 'affect' a tribunal's exercise or purported exercise of power if the erroneous finding forms the basis of the decision or is an element in the process of reasoning that led to the decision.

3   Insofar as administrative tribunals are concerned, a jurisdictional error of the *Anisminic* type will be committed by such a body where the error is such that the body's exercise or purported exercise of power is thereby affected.

As was pointed out in *Minister for Immigration and Multicultural Affairs v Yusuf* (2001), it is necessary, however, to understand what is meant by 'jurisdictional error' under the general law and the consequences that follow from a decision maker making such an error. 'Jurisdictional error' can, according to *Craig*, be seen to embrace a number of different kinds of error, the list of which in *Craig* (see above) is not, according to *Yusuf*, exhaustive. Those different kinds of error may well overlap. The circumstances of a particular case may permit more than one characterisation of the error identified, such as the decision maker both asking the wrong question and ignoring relevant material. What is important, however, is that identifying a wrong issue, asking a wrong question, ignoring relevant material or relying on irrelevant material (the errors identified in the list in *Craig*) in a way that affects the exercise of power is to make an error of law. Further, doing so results in the decision maker exceeding the authority or powers given by the relevant statute. In other words, if an error of those types is made, the decision maker did not have authority to make the decision that was made; he or she did not have jurisdiction to make it.

Australian courts had developed, well before *Anisminic*, a fairly liberal interpretation of the traditional doctrine of jurisdictional error, and can, and often do, achieve a very similar result to the *Anisminic* doctrine by:

- generally avoiding, when dealing with a judicial or quasi-judicial body, the language and thought-forms of extended *ultra vires* (in particular, 'irrelevant considerations'); and
- seeking to find what is sometimes referred to as a 'constructive jurisdictional error': see *ex p Hebburn Ltd; Re Kearsley Shire Council* (1947).

Thus, if an inferior tribunal misunderstands the nature of the jurisdiction which it is to exercise, and proceeds to:

- 'apply a wrong and inadmissible test': see *Estate and Trust Agencies (1927) Ltd v Singapore Improvement Trust* (1937);
- 'misconceive its duty, or function, or the nature of its task': see *R v War Pensions Entitlement Appeal Tribunal ex p Bott* (1933);
- 'not apply itself to the question which the law prescribes' or 'ask the wrong question': see *Bott*; *R v Booth ex p Administrative and Clerical Officers' Association* (1978); or
- 'misunderstand the nature of the opinion which it is to form': see *R v Connell ex p Hetton Bellbird Collieries Ltd* (1944),

the tribunal's decision will be a purported and not a real exercise of jurisdiction, leaving the jurisdiction in law 'constructively unexercised' (see *ex p Hebburn Ltd v Kearsley Shire Council* (1947)).

In addition, a tribunal may fall into jurisdictional error if it:

- ignores relevant material or relies on irrelevant material, for example, in forming any 'opinion' required to be formed as a prerequisite to the proper exercise of its jurisdiction: see *Connell*; or
- rejects evidence or makes a decision unsupported by the evidence: see *R v Australian Stevedoring Industry Board ex p Melbourne Stevedoring Co Ltd* (1953); or
- makes an erroneous finding or reaches a mistaken conclusion, where the *only* conclusion available on the evidence is that the primary facts, fully found, are necessarily within or outside a statutory description, and a contrary conclusion has been made: see *Hope v Bathurst City Council* (1980),

in such a way as to indicate that the tribunal misunderstood the test it had to apply in determining matters going to its jurisdiction, or in exercising its jurisdiction, with the result that the tribunal's exercise or purported exercise of power was thereby fundamentally affected: see *Craig v South Australia* (1995); *Coal and Allied Operations Pty Ltd v Australian Industrial Relations Commission* (2000).

Case example

A board was empowered by statute to cancel or suspend the registration of an employer engaged in the stevedoring industry where, after such inquiry as it thought fit, the board was satisfied that the employer was 'unfit to continue to be registered as an employer' or had 'acted in a manner whereby the proper performance of stevedoring operations ha[d] been interfered with'.

A company, a registered employer under the statute, was made the subject of an inquiry by a duly authorised delegate of the board on the general ground that it had not exercised proper supervision over waterside workers employed by it.

The High Court of Australia held that the board must understand correctly the test provided or prescribed by the statute and actually apply it, and went on to say that if on the facts no basis could exist for exercising the power it would be a proper exercise of the court's jurisdiction to intervene. It was not, however, enough if the board or its delegate, properly interpreting the statute and applying the correct test, nevertheless was satisfied on inadequate material that facts existed which in truth would fulfil the statutory conditions. The inadequacy of material was not in itself a ground for intervention, although it might support an inference that the board applied the wrong test or was not in reality satisfied of the requisite matters. If there are other conditions that that was so or that the purpose of the function committed to the tribunal was misconceived, it is but a short step to the conclusion that in truth the power has not arisen because the conditions for its exercise do not exist in law and in fact.

The board was found to have resorted to the power to cancel or suspend merely as a means of enforcing upon employers the requirement to maintain a supervision of gangs of waterside workers to ensure that the members did not cease or suspend work or leave the ship or wharf without discovery and that their absence was reported. The Court stated that a jurisdictional error would be committed by such a tribunal where it either rejected evidence or made a decision unsupported by the evidence *in such a way* as to indicate that it had misunderstood the test it had to apply in determining matters going to jurisdiction, applied the wrong test or was not in reality satisfied as to the requisite matters. The board was found to have made a decision unsupported by the evidence in such a way as to indicate that it had misunderstood the relevant statutory test.

R v Australian Stevedoring Industry Board
ex p Melbourne Stevedoring Co Pty Ltd (1953)

More recently, the NSW Court of Appeal has tended to apply a fairly traditional view of jurisdictional error, despite *Craig*: see, for example, *Newcastle Wallsend Coal Co Pty Ltd v Court of Coal Mines Regulation* (1997); *Londish v Knox Grammar School* (1997); *Woolworths Ltd v Hawke* (1998).

In the context of the Administrative Decisions (Judicial Review) Act 1977 (Cth), a decision to which that Act applies may be reviewed under that Act on, relevantly, the ground that the decision involved an error of law:

- whether jurisdictional or non-jurisdictional; and
- whether or not the error appears on the record: see s 5(1)(f) of that Act. (See Chapter 8.)

Fact

'Ordinary' fact –
UNREVIEWABLE

Jurisdictional fact –
REVIEWABLE* as
jurisdictional error of law

Law

Jurisdictional error –
REVIEWABLE*

Error of law on face of the record – REVIEWABLE*

'Anisminic' error –
REVIEWABLE* *if*:
(a) administrative tribunal
   (cf inferior court); and
(b) exercise, or purported
   exercise, of power
   thereby affected

* *Subject to privative clause*

Privative clauses

Introduction

Privative (or 'ouster') clauses are attempts by the legislature to prevent or otherwise restrict judicial review of administrative decisions.

The clauses are construed by reference to a presumption that the legislature does not intend to deprive the citizen of access to the courts, other than to the extent expressly stated or necessarily to be implied: see *Clancy v Butchers' Shop Employees Union* (1904); *Anisminic Ltd v Foreign Compensation Commission* (1969); *Hockey v Yelland* (1984).

Only if the legislature speaks in the clearest of terms will the courts assume a legislative intent to preclude the operation of the doctrine of judicial review, and even then only to the extent expressly stated or necessarily to be implied.

Privative clauses in the federal sphere

The High Court cannot be deprived of its supervisory jurisdiction to grant relief of the kinds referred to in s 75(v) of the Commonwealth Constitution.

Section 75(v) of the Constitution provides that the High Court has original jurisdiction in all matters in which 'a writ of mandamus or prohibition, or an injunction is sought against an officer of the Commonwealth'.

The expression 'officer of the Commonwealth' will include all Australian Public Service Officers and members of federal administrative tribunals (but not State or local government officials or employees): see *R v Murray and Cormie ex p Commonwealth* (1916); *R v Drake-Brockman ex p National Oil Pty Ltd* (1943).

See also s 4 of the Administrative Decisions (Judicial Review) Act 1977 which provides that, to the extent to which a privative clause in existence immediately before the commencement of that Act (1 October 1980) would prevent or otherwise restrict review under that Act, the clause will be ineffective (see Chapter 8).

In *Plaintiff S157/2002 v Commonwealth of Australia* (2003), the High Court of Australia held that certain privative clause provisions contained in the Migration Act 1958 (Cth), which purported to prevent judicial review of virtually every 'decision' made, proposed to be made or required to be made, as the case may be, under that Act or under a regulation or other instrument made under that Act (see s 474 of that Act), were not apt to refer to decisions *purportedly* made under that Act. The Court held that, if the statutory provisions were to be so construed, they would be in direct conflict with s 75(v) of the Commonwealth Constitution. Further, they would confer authority on a non-judicial decision maker of the Commonwealth to determine conclusively the limits of its own jurisdiction and, thus, at least in some cases, infringe the mandate implicit in the text of Chapter III of the Constitution that the judicial power of the Commonwealth be exercised only by the courts named and referred to in s 71. Thus, the privative clause provisions in the Migration Act 1958 (Cth) were held not to extend to prevent judicial review of decisions involving jurisdictional error.

Types of privative clauses

Privative clauses take various forms.

Finality clauses

A privative clause which merely purports to make a decision 'final' or 'not subject to appeal' will not prevent the use of certiorari for either jurisdictional error or non-jurisdictional error of law on the face of the record: see *R v Medical Appeal Tribunal ex p Gilmore* (1957); *Anisminic Ltd v Foreign Compensation Commission* (1969), unless the clause is also clearly expressed to protect 'purported decisions': see *R v Commissioner of Police (NT) ex p Holroyd* (1965).

'No certiorari' ('shall not be questioned') clauses

Use of certiorari (or prohibition, or both) to quash a voidable non-jurisdictional error of law apparent on the face of the record may be defeated by a suitably worded privative clause, in particular a so called 'no certiorari' or 'shall not be questioned' clause: see *South East Asia Fire Bricks Sdn Bhd v Non-Metallic Mineral Products Manufacturing Employees Union* (1981); *Houssein v Under Secretary of Industrial Relations and Technology (NSW)* (1982).

Time limit privative clauses

This type of limited privative clause purports to exclude judicial review of the validity of an administrative decision:

- only after the expiration of a certain time limit (for example, three months); and
- in some cases, only if 'proper' public notice of the making of the decision is given by the decision maker.

A time limit privative clause:

- is analogous to a statute of limitations; and
- ordinarily precludes judicial review once the stipulated time period has expired.

In *North Sydney Municipal Council v Lycenko & Associates Pty Ltd* (1988), Mahoney JA stated that:

- it was 'beyond question' that such a clause precluded any challenge after the expiration of the specified time period; and

- in that regard, there was 'no distinction between defects of form and defects of substance': see also *R v Secretary of State for the Environment ex p Ostler* (1977).

Nevertheless, until fairly recently, the preponderance of judicial authority (see *Woolworths Ltd v Bathurst City Council* (1987); *Darkingung Local Aboriginal Land Council v Minister for Natural Resources (No 2)* (1987); *Yadle Investments Pty Ltd v RTA of NSW* (1991); *Darkingung Local Aboriginal Land Council v Minister Administering the Crown Lands Act* (1991)) was to the effect that a time limit privative clause would preclude a challenge after the expiration of the specified time period on the ground that the decision maker:

- took into account irrelevant matters;
- failed to take into account relevant matters;
- reached a decision not reasonably open to it in the relevant sense; or
- acted with 'manifest unreasonableness'.

However, such a clause would not preclude challenge where any of the aforementioned errors was material to bad faith.

In addition, a time limit privative clause:

- Will not preclude a challenge after the expiration of the specified time period where the decision was 'manifestly *ultra vires* or in excess of jurisdiction'.

  'Manifest jurisdictional error or *ultra vires*' refers to an error of law which is 'readily understood or perceived by the eye ... evident and obvious ... appear[ing] plainly on the face of the instrument': see *Darkingung Local Aboriginal Land Council v Minister for Natural Resources (No 2)* (1987), *per* Stein J.

- Might not (and probably would not) preclude a challenge after the expiration of the specified time period on the ground that the decision maker acted in bad faith.

- Might not (and almost certainly would not) preclude a challenge after the expiration of the specified time period, where the challenge was based on a breach of the rules of procedural fairness: see *Worimi Local Aboriginal Land Council v Minister Administering the Crown Lands Act* (1991); cf *Darkingung Local Aboriginal Land Council v Minister for Natural Resources (No 2)* (1987) (overruled insofar as it was authority for the proposition that judicial review of the certificate was excluded on the ground of denial of procedural fairness).

However, in *Coles Supermarkets Australia Pty Ltd v Minister for Urban Affairs and Planning* (1996), Pearlman J, in the Land and Environment Court of NSW, relying on the approach of the High Court in *R v Hickman ex p Fox and Clinton* (1945) and various other authorities, and distinguishing such cases as *Woolworths Ltd v Bathurst City Council* (1987) and *Worimi Local Aboriginal Land Council v Minister Administering the Crown Lands Act* (1991), held that a time limit privative clause will operate to exclude a judicial challenge on the ground of denial or breach of the rules of procedural fairness, except where the tests enunciated in *Hickman* are not satisfied. In that regard, Dixon J (as he then was) in *Hickman* enunciated the following principle (now usually referred to as the '*Hickman* principle') commonly applied in the federal sphere:

> Such a clause is interpreted as meaning that no decision which is in fact given by the body concerned shall be invalidated on the ground that it has not conformed to the requirements governing its proceedings or the exercise of its authority or has not confined its acts within the limits laid down by the instrument giving it authority, provided always that its decision is a *bona fide* attempt to exercise its power, that it relates to the subject matter of the legislation, and that it is reasonably capable of reference to the power given to the body.

See, in addition, *Breitkopf v Wyong Council* (1996) in which Bignold J, also in the Land and Environment Court of NSW, adopting a different view of the relevance of the authorities from that expressed by Pearlman J in the *Coles Supermarkets* case, gave the time limit privative clause in question full effect, stating that, in his opinion, there was (contrary to some earlier decisions of the Land and Environment Court such as *Woolworths Ltd v Bathurst City Council*) no justification for reading down the plain meaning of the provision to allow for any implied exceptions.

More recently, the NSW Court of Appeal has applied the *Hickman* principle in a number of important cases, including *Londish v Knox Grammar School* (1997).

Ground limit privative clauses

Another type of privative clause is one which is expressed to limit judicial review to certain specified grounds (for example, denial of procedural fairness, lack of jurisdiction): see *Jet 60 Minute Cleaners Pty Ltd v Brownette* (1981); *Public Service Association of South Australia v Federated Clerks' Union of Australia, South Australian Branch* (1991).

6 Remedies and Standing

> **You should be familiar with the following areas:**
>
> - the availability of the common law remedies (former prerogative writs) of certiorari, prohibition, mandamus and *quo warranto*
> - the availability of the equitable remedies of injunction and declaration
> - the requirements as to standing

Relief in the nature of certiorari and prohibition

Introduction

Relief in the nature of certiorari exists in several forms. In its usual form, certiorari is an order from a superior court to:

- remove the official record of an administrative authority or tribunal or inferior court into the superior court for judicial review; and
- quash (expunge or set aside) the decision of the inferior body, in the event that the superior court finds that the decision was *ultra vires* or was otherwise made in want or excess of jurisdiction or that there was a breach of the rules of procedural fairness or fraud.

Relief in the nature of prohibition is an order from a superior court which restrains an administrative authority or tribunal from:

- entering upon a matter; or
- proceeding further with a matter,

which lies beyond its power, authority or jurisdiction.

Availability of relief

Relief in the nature of certiorari and prohibition will lie:

> ... wherever any body of persons having legal authority to determine questions affecting the rights of subjects, and having the duty to act judicially, act in excess of their legal authority.
>
> *R v Electricity Commissioners ex p London Electricity Joint Committee* (1924), *per* Atkin LJ

Lord Justice Atkin's *dictum* is still the *locus classicus* for the availability of the two remedies, but over the years there have been some judicial refinements:

- As to the question of when a body has 'legal authority', the courts now appear to be moving to a position where the essential question is not the formal source of power to determine rights, but whether the authority being exercised is sufficiently 'public' in nature: see *R v City Panel on Takeovers and Mergers ex p Datafin plc* (1987). In the past, relief was held to be unavailable where the body in question was a private or domestic body or where the matter complained of was a private law matter of a public body: see *R v BBC ex p Lavelle* (1983).

- The requirement as to 'rights' was relaxed quite early to allow the remedies to lie where rights in the strict legal sense (for example, proprietary rights) were not actually being determined by the body in question.

  However, it is still generally considered necessary that the 'determination' in question create or affect rights and obligations in some substantive way (see *R v Collins ex p ACTU-Solo Enterprises Pty Ltd* (1976); *Greiner v ICAC/Moore v ICAC* (1992)), even if the particular decision is not the final or ultimate one.

  In contrast, in *Hot Holdings Pty Ltd v Creasy* (1996), it was held that a preliminary decision or recommendation, if it is one to which regard must be paid by the final decision maker, would have the requisite legal effect upon rights to attract certiorari.

- The duty to act 'judicially' is now interpreted as a duty to act fairly in the making of administrative decisions affecting rights, interests and legitimate expectations: see *Ridge v Baldwin* (1964); *Kioa v West* (1985).

Standing

Originally, the test of standing to seek relief in the nature of certiorari or prohibition was 'person aggrieved'.

A person had to show that he or she had suffered damage to some interest greater than that of ordinary members of the public. Such a person had legal standing, as of right, to seek relief in the nature of certiorari and prohibition: see *R v Surrey JJ* (1870).

Administrative law remedies

Common law remedies:

Certiorari	calls up the record for review, quashes decision if made outside jurisdiction
Prohibition	restrains decision maker from exceeding its powers
Mandamus	commands performance of a lawful public duty
Quo warranto	restrains disentitled person from acting in a public office

Equitable remedies:

Injunction	restrains commission or continuance of a wrongful act
	OR directs the doing of something which ought to be done
Declaration	creates, preserves, asserts or testifies to a legal right

Damages:

Misfeasance in	provides for recovery of damages in respect of *public office* for an intentional and wrongful act on the part of a public official

A 'person aggrieved' by a decision did not have to be a party to the actual decision: see *R v Hendon RDC ex p Chorley* (1933).

In all other cases, the court had a discretion as to whether or not to grant relief to a 'stranger' and would generally only do so where it felt that a matter of sufficient public importance was at stake: see *R v Stafford JJ ex p Stafford Corporation* (1940).

In more recent years, the test of 'special interest' (see *Australian Conservation Foundation Inc v Commonwealth* (1980)), applicable to actions for equitable relief, has (in the absence of a right of statutory standing) sometimes been applied: see, for example, *Mirror Newspapers Ltd v Waller* (1985); *State Planning Commission ex p Helena Valley/Boya Assoc Inc* (1990).

In the absence of a statutory right of standing (see s 123 of the Environmental Planning and Assessment Act 1979 (NSW)), a person has a special interest in the subject matter of the proceedings for the purposes of relief in the nature of certiorari and prohibition if the person's interests may be prejudicially affected in some way and the person is someone other than a 'mere busybody': see *R v Liverpool Corporation ex p Liverpool Taxi Fleet Operators' Association* (1972); *R v Greater London Council ex p Blackburn* (1976); *R v Corporation of the City of Burnside ex p Ipswich Properties Pty Ltd* (1987).

Relief by way of mandamus

Introduction

An order by way of mandamus is used to compel a person or body to perform a lawful 'public duty'.

Availability of relief

For relief by way of mandamus to be available, three requirements must be satisfied:

1   there must be a 'duty' to be performed;
2   the duty must be a 'public' one;
3   the duty must be 'lawful'.

'Duty'

There must be a 'duty' to be performed, that is, some act that is required to be performed or some decision that is required to be made.

In *Ainsworth and Another v Criminal Justice Commission* (1992), it was held that relief by way of mandamus was inappropriate as the

Commission was under no statutory duty to investigate and report upon the matter complained of.

Mandamus will also not lie so as to dictate the manner in which a statutory discretionary power is to be exercised: see *Randall v Northcote Corporation* (1910). Where the duty involves the exercise of a discretion, the court will only see that the discretion is exercised.

Where there has been an abuse of power, the court may take the view that there has been no exercise of the discretion and will require that the authority in question address itself to the question of the exercise of the discretion and exercise the discretionary power according to law: see *ex p SF Bowser & Co ex p Randwick Municipal Council* (1927); *Dickinson v Perrignon* (1973).

Where there has been any misconception or misunderstanding (on the part of the decision maker) as to the nature or extent of the duty to be performed, relief by way of mandamus will lie: see *Sinclair v Mining Warden at Maryborough* (1975).

'Public duty'

The duty in question must be a 'public' one.

Relief will not lie to control the activities of public bodies in respect of their private duties. However, in recent years it has become increasingly difficult to distinguish between what is 'public' and what is 'private': see *John Fairfax & Sons Ltd v Australian Telecommunications Commission* (1977); *Della-Vedova v State Energy Commission of Western Australia* (1990).

'Lawful duty'

The duty must be a 'lawful' one.

There must have been both a demand for its performance and a refusal to perform the duty: see *R v Brecknock and Abergavenny Canal Co* (1935); *R v City of Preston ex p Sandringham Drive-In Theatre Pty Ltd* (1965). A 'conditional agreement' to perform the duty may or may not amount to a refusal: see *Brecknock*. Much depends on each particular case. Undue delay can be treated as refusal to act. However, what constitutes undue delay will also vary by context.

Discretionary considerations

Relief by way of mandamus is highly discretionary, indeed more so than relief in the nature of certiorari and prohibition, since it is not available as of right: see *Commissioner for Local Government Lands and Settlement v Kaderbhai* (1931).

The court's discretion, though wide, is still to be exercised 'judicially': see *Stepney Borough v John Walker & Sons Ltd* (1934).

Relief by way of mandamus:

- may be refused on the ground of delay (see *Ku-ring-gai Municipal Council v Arthur H Gillott Pty Ltd* (1968)), or where it would be unnecessary or futile;

- will generally be refused where there is an alternative remedy of law (for example, right of appeal) which is equally convenient, beneficial and effectual: see *Re Barlow (Rector of Ewhurst)* (1861); *Perpetual Executors & Trustees Assoc of Australia Ltd v Hosken* (1912); *Tooth & Co Ltd v Parramatta City Council* (1955); *ex p Mullen; Re Wigley* (1970); *Bilbao v Farquhar* (1974);

- will certainly be refused where the application for relief is not made in good faith or is made to achieve some ulterior purpose: see *ex p Commissioner for Railways; Re Locke* (1968).

Standing

Originally, the common law test for standing for mandamus was stricter than that for relief in the nature of certiorari and prohibition, in that it was necessary for the plaintiff to show that he or she had a legal right to enforce the public duty in question: see *R v Guardians of Lewisham Union* (1897).

In more recent years, the test of 'special interest' has, in the absence of a statutory right of standing, been applied, at least in NSW, to actions for relief in the form of both certiorari and mandamus: see *Mirror Newspapers Ltd v Waller* (1985).

In other jurisdictions, the 'sufficient interest' test of standing formulated by Lord Wilberforce in *Inland Revenue Commissioners v National Federation of Self-Employed & Small Business Ltd* (1982) has been applied: see *West Australian Field & Game Assoc v Pearce* (1992).

At common law, a person is *prima facie* entitled to relief in the nature of mandamus if the person can show that the subject of the duty directly affects him or her: see *R v Commissioner of Police of the Metropolis ex p Blackburn* (1968); *Bilbao v Farquhar* (1974).

Relief in the nature of *quo warranto*

Introduction

Originally, the ancient writ of *quo warranto* ('by what authority') was available for use by the Crown to protect the Crown against encroachment on the royal prerogative or any rights, franchises or liberties of the Crown.

The writ subsequently fell into disuse and was replaced by the practice of filing an 'information in the nature of a writ of *quo warranto*' by the Attorney General.

Relief in the nature of *quo warranto* is discussed generally by Dixon CJ in *Liston v Davies* (1957).

Availability of relief

Relief in the nature of *quo warranto*, which lies for usurping any public, substantive office (for example, a local government civic office), now takes various forms, depending upon the particular jurisdiction.

For example, s 70 of the Supreme Court Act 1970 (NSW) provides that where any person acts in an office in which that person is not entitled to act and an information in the nature of *quo warranto* would, but for s 12 of the Act (which abolished the former writ), lie against that person, the Supreme Court may grant an injunction restraining the person from so acting and may (if the case so requires) declare the office to be vacant.

Discretionary considerations

The remedy is discretionary and will not usually be granted where other proceedings, relevantly, 'ouster' proceedings (for example, s 329 of the Local Government Act 1993 (NSW)), are available: see *R v Morton* (1892).

Any delay in seeking relief will need to be adequately explained.

The conduct of the person seeking relief may be examined by the court: see *R v Boyd ex p Saville* (1868); *ex p Reay* (1876); *ex p Gale; Re McMaster* (1891).

Standing

At common law, a person seeking relief in the nature of *quo warranto* had to show an interest (now presumably a 'special interest') in the particular matter, for example, being a resident of the local government area.

Injunctions

Introduction

An injunction is a court order which:

- restrains the commission or continuance of a wrongful act (known as a 'prohibitory ['restrictive' or 'preventive'] injunction'); or
- directs the doing of something which ought to be done (known as a 'mandatory ['compulsive'] injunction').

An injunction may be:
- 'perpetual', that is, it is granted at the conclusion of the court proceedings; or
- 'interlocutory' (or 'interim'), that is, it is granted before or during the proceedings to prevent any change in the status quo until a final determination is made by the court.

There are also other types of injunctions, including:

- a *quia timet* injunction, which is granted where the plaintiff has reasonable grounds to fear that the defendant may infringe the plaintiff's rights;
- a 'Mareva injunction', which is an order restraining the defendant, or potential defendant, from disposing of his or her assets, being assets which may be required to satisfy the plaintiff's claim (in respect of which there is a *prima facie* cause of action): see *Nippon Yusen Kaisha v Karageorgis* (1975); *Mareva Compania Naviera SA v International Bulk Carriers SA* (1975); *Jackson v Sterling Industries* (1987); and
- an 'Anton Piller order', which is a special type of mandatory injunction (as well as being a form of discovery) enabling a plaintiff, without the prior knowledge of the defendant, but with his or her permission (ordered by the court), to enter the defendant's premises and search for, inspect and take copies of documents and other things essential to the plaintiff's impending litigation (in certain types of proceedings), being documents and things which might otherwise be destroyed by the defendant or removed from the court's jurisdiction: see *Anton Piller KG v*

Manufacturing Processes Ltd (1976); *Columbia Pictures Inc v Robinson* (1987).

Availability of relief

The courts are generally slow to grant injunctive relief against public administrative bodies except in the case of *ultra vires*, jurisdictional error or denial of procedural fairness: see *Grand Junction Waterworks Co v Hampton Urban District Council* (1898); *M v Statutory Committee of the Queensland Law Society* (1973); *Ewert v Lonie* (1972).

Injunctions are generally directed towards requiring or preventing future events, which would themselves be wrongful (in a broad sense). Those future events must, by evidence in the case, be shown to be reasonably probable; and the usual way of doing this is to lead evidence of actions performed in the past by the defendant. However, when the probability of some future wrong is established, it is to this future state of affairs that the order is directed: see *Attrill v Richmond River Shire Council* (1993).

Mandatory injunctions are much less common in public law, as relief by way of mandamus is normally a more appropriate remedy: see *Sinclair v Mining Warden at Maryborough* (1975).

An undertaking as to damages (that is, an undertaking that if the interlocutory relief is later dissolved, the plaintiff will compensate the defendant for any loss caused by the injunction) ordinarily will be required of a person seeking interlocutory relief: see *Gillette v Diamond Edge* (1926).

However, in relation to public interest environmental litigation, even if the applicant for relief is unwilling or unable to give an undertaking as to damages, that will not necessarily be fatal to the application: see *Ross v State Rail Authority of NSW* (1987).

Discretionary considerations

The equitable remedies of injunction and declaration, and the common law remedies in the nature of the former prerogative writs of certiorari, prohibition, mandamus and *quo warranto*, are all discretionary remedies.

Injunctive relief is, however, highly discretionary: see *Queensland v Commonwealth* (1988).

The court will have regard to a number of factors, including:

- the conduct of the applicant for relief (including whether or not the applicant has expressly or impliedly acquiesced in the act or omission sought to be remedied);
- whether the applicant has acted promptly in seeking relief;
- the hardship which would be caused to the defendant;
- the triviality (or otherwise) of the matter (including whether or not the act or omission sought to be remedied was the result of a deliberate flouting of the law or simply a misunderstanding as to legal obligations);
- whether the granting of the relief would be futile or unnecessary;
- the availability of alternative remedies (and their effectiveness or otherwise);
- any adverse implications for the public generally (for example, environmental planning implications arising from the carrying out of the unauthorised development), and so forth.

The discretion to be exercised in injunctive proceedings involves the 'weighing up' of all relevant factors – not only the public interest, but also the rights and interests of the parties including matters of conduct, hardship and convenience: see *Warringah Shire Council v Sedevcic* (1987).

The court 'must decide to do what is fair and just as between the parties and in the public interest': see *Rowley v NSW Leather Trading Co Pty Ltd* (1980), *per* Cripps J.

Where there is a statutory remedy available, the court will construe the statutory provision to ascertain whether the statutory remedy was intended to be exclusive: see *North Sydney Municipal Council v Comfytex Pty Ltd* (1975).

A court may refuse injunctive relief – especially in the areas of public law – where to grant the injunction would work such an injustice as to be disproportionate to the end secured by enforcement of the law: see *Strathfield Municipal Council v Alpha Plastics Pty Ltd* (1988).

Standing

Originally, a plaintiff could sue for injunctive (and declaratory) relief – without joining the Attorney General, in two cases:

1   where the interference with the public right was such that some private right of the plaintiff was at the same time interfered with; or

2   where no private right was interfered with, but the plaintiff suffered 'special and peculiar damage' (in pecuniary terms).

See *Boyce v Paddington Borough Council* (1903), *per* Buckley J (affirmed by the House of Lords (1906)).

In Australia, in the absence of a statutory right of standing, before a private plaintiff can institute injunctive proceedings, the person must now show, in the absence of some right being affected, that he or she has a 'special interest' in the subject matter of the action: see *Australian Conservation Foundation Inc v Commonwealth* (*ACF* case) (1980); *Onus v Alcoa of Australia Ltd* (1981).

A 'special interest':

*   may involve some actual or apprehended injury or damage to the person's property or proprietary rights, to his or her business or economic interests: see *New South Wales Fish Authority v Phillips* (1970), or perhaps to his or her social, political or spiritual interests: see *Onus; Ogle v Strickland* (1987); but

*   must be more than 'a mere intellectual or emotional concern': see *ACF* case.

Case example

> Two members of a particular Aboriginal community sought injunctive and declaratory relief to prevent a company from building an aluminium smelter on land containing Aboriginal relics, in alleged contravention of certain legislation which made it an offence to damage or otherwise interfere with such relics. The appellants were, according to Aboriginal laws and customs, the custodians of the relics. The relics were stated to be of great cultural and spiritual significance to them, as they were used to teach Aboriginal culture to their children. The High Court of Australia held that the appellants had a 'special interest' in the subject matter of the proceedings.
>
> *Onus v Alcoa of Australia Ltd* (1981)

Where a statute creates a criminal offence, injunctive or declaratory relief cannot be claimed by a private person suing alone, in the absence of:

*   a 'special interest'; or

- some special damage suffered by the person in addition to the offence against the public at large: see *ex p Island Records Ltd* (1978); or

- a statutory right of standing,

except, perhaps, in respect of flagrant and repeated (and, unless restrained, likely to be further repeated) breaches of the law: see *Cooney v Ku-ring-gai Municipal Council* (1963).

Generally speaking, however, the Attorney General is the appropriate person to bring all such proceedings, either on his or her own motion or by relator: see *Gouriet v Union of Post Office Workers* (1978); *ACF* case (1980).

The balance of judicial authority is to the effect that the Attorney General's discretion in relation to the exercise of his or her fiat is absolute and non-reviewable: see *Gouriet; ACF* case.

Declarations

Introduction

A declaration, or declaratory judgment or order, is a court order which creates, preserves, asserts or testifies to the existence of a legal right or duty or the correct legal position between the parties.

The modern use of the declaration against public authorities such as local councils can be generally traced to *Dyson v Attorney General* (1911).

Availability of relief

A declaration is a broad based and flexible remedy which is commonly used by superior courts.

Declaratory relief is available in a wide range of situations, including questions of *ultra vires*, denial of procedural fairness, and questions concerning whether, in a particular case, there is a duty to act.

Scope of the remedy

A declaration may be sought and granted:

- to the effect that only part of an administrative decision or action is invalid, provided the invalid part can be separated from the rest of the decision or action;

- in conjunction with some other remedy (for example, an injunction);

- irrespective of whether or not consequential relief is, or can be, claimed: see s 75 of the Supreme Court Act 1970 (NSW).

Discretionary considerations

The court has a wide discretion as to whether to grant or refuse declaratory relief: see *Ibeneweka v Egbuna* (1964); *Sutherland Shire Council v Leyendekkers* (1970); *Forster v Jododex Australia Pty Ltd* (1972); *Johnco Nominees Pty Ltd v Albury-Wodonga (NSW) Corporation* (1977).

It is neither possible nor desirable to fetter the court's broad discretion by laying down rules as to the manner of its exercise: see *Forster v Jododex Australia Pty Ltd* (1972).

In *Russian Commercial and Industrial Bank v British Bank for Foreign Trade Ltd* (1921), Lord Dunedin set out the rules which should in general be satisfied before the discretion is exercised in favour of a grant of declaratory relief:

> The question must be real and not a theoretical question; the person raising it must have a real interest to raise it; he must be able to secure a proper contradictor, that is to say, someone presently existing who has a true interest to oppose the declaration sought.

Lord Dunedin's *dictum* has been interpreted as follows:

- The 'question' may be one of fact or law, but must not be merely 'abstract' or purely 'hypothetical': see *Johnco Nominees Pty Ltd v Albury-Wodonga (NSW) Corporation* (1977); *Ainsworth v Criminal Justice Commission* (1992).

- There must be a 'real' legal controversy between the parties, such that the rights and interests of the respective parties depend upon its resolution.

- A party with a present stand of neutrality, or who is simply prepared to abide by any order which the court might make, can still be a 'proper contradictor', provided the party has a 'true interest' in the other side's claim: see *Oil Basins Ltd v Commonwealth* (1993).

Declaratory relief may be refused on the grounds of futility unless there is some special reason for intervention by the court (for example, unavoidable detriment), where there is, in existence, a special tribunal which has been established by statute, with its own special procedures, to specifically determine the respective rights and obligations of the parties: see *Forster v Jododex Australia Pty Ltd* (1972); *Pyx Granite Co Ltd v Ministry of Housing and Local Government* (1960).

Case example

> The Land and Environment Court of NSW, in previous proceedings (see *Byron Shire Businesses for the Future Inc v Byron Council* (the *Club Med* case) (1994)), had declared null and void a development consent purportedly granted by a local council. The developer then instituted separate proceedings seeking certain declaratory relief in relation to the legal status of the original development application lodged with the council and the designation of the proposed development. The court granted declaratory relief (as to the status of a development application) in circumstances where the council's position was largely one of neutrality, together with a preparedness to abide by any order which the court might make. However, the court refused to grant declaratory relief in relation to the question of whether the proposed development constituted 'designated development' within the meaning of the salient legislation on the grounds that, firstly, to grant such relief would be 'premature' in all the circumstances, and, secondly, that the particular issue had not been fully dealt with in the subject proceedings. Thus, the court concluded that it would be of no utility to make the second declaration sought.
>
> *Holiday Villages (Byron Bay) Pty Ltd v Byron Council* (1995)

Declaratory relief will almost certainly be refused where, for example, the party seeking the relief has elected to treat the decision complained of as valid by appealing from it in preference to asserting his or her rights to pursue judicial review: see *Ableton Management Pty Ltd v Gosford City Council* (1994).

Standing

In the absence of a statutory right of standing, the relevant test for standing is the same as for injunctive relief (see above), that is, a 'special interest' in the subject matter of the action: see *Australian Conservation Foundation Inc v Commonwealth* (1980).

Damages

Introduction

In addition to the invocation, in an appropriate case, of any one or more of the common law or equitable remedies discussed above, an affected person may have an action for damages against a decision maker.

Actions 'on the case'

Until fairly recently, it was possible for a plaintiff to claim damages – independently of trespass, negligence or nuisance – from, relevantly, a public authority in an action 'on the case', where the plaintiff suffered harm or loss as the inevitable consequence of an:

- unlawful;
- intentional; and
- positive,

act of the authority.

This was known as the *'Beaudesert* principle': see *Beaudesert Shire Council v Smith* (1966); *Hull v Canterbury Municipal Council* (1974).

The High Court, in 1995, overruled *Beaudesert* in the case of *Northern Territory v Mengel* (1995), having concluded that *Beaudesert* was too broad as it purported to create liability without negligence.

Misfeasance in a public office

This common law tort is available where a person suffers purely economic loss as a result of an:

- intentional; and
- wrongful act,

on the part of a public official (or 'public officer'): see *Farrington v Thomson and Bridgland* (1959); *Campbell v Ramsay* (1968); *Tampion v Anderson* (1973); *Pemberton v Attorney General* (1978); *Dunlop v Woollahra Municipal Council* (1981). A local council is a public officer for the purposes of this tort action: see *Dunlop*.

The plaintiff must establish that:

- The defendant is a public officer, that is, the holder of a public office, being someone who:

- ⊃ is paid out of public funds; and
- ⊃ owes duties to members of the public as to how the office shall be exercised.
- The defendant *knowingly*, whether or not maliciously, committed an intentional and wrongful act amounting to an abuse of his or her office.
- The plaintiff was a member of the public to whom the defendant owed a duty not to commit the particular abuse complained of.
- The plaintiff suffered pure economic loss as a result of that act. The tort of misfeasance in public office:
  - ⊃ has a limited scope as public officers are liable for general negligence;
  - ⊃ is limited to acts:
    - – *intended* to cause harm, and
    - – knowingly, or recklessly, performed without power: see *Northern Territory v Mengel* (1995); and
  - ⊃ provides for the recovery of damages, including (probably) exemplary damages: cf *Farrington v Thomson and Bridgland* (1959).

7 Public Interest Immunity

> You should be familiar with the following areas:
>
> - the nature of 'public interest immunity'
> - the difference between a 'class' claim and a 'contents' claim
> - the competing aspects of the 'public interest'

Introduction

'Public interest immunity', formerly known as 'Crown privilege', is a principle whereby disclosure of otherwise admissible documents or information may be denied or excluded because the balance of the public interest so requires.

The immunity is both a rule of evidence and part of our constitutional law (being an aspect of the so called 'shield of the Crown': see *Mersey Docks and Harbour Trustees v Cameron* (1865); *Young v Quin* (1985). It operates in a manner similar to legal professional privilege, but it is not a privilege *per se*.

The expression 'Crown privilege' is also no longer apposite as other 'secrets' have been protected under the rule: see *D v National Society for the Prevention of Cruelty to Children* (*D's* case) (1978); *Aboriginal Sacred Sites Protection Authority v Maurice* (1986).

The categories of public interest are not closed: see *D's* case. However, the courts are cautious in extending heads of claim to withhold evidence required for the administration of justice: see *Aboriginal Sacred Sites*.

The scope and nature of the immunity

The scope and nature of public interest immunity are as follows:

- The immunity is a narrow one, to be exercised only where there is some plain overriding principle of public policy: see *Robinson v South Australia (No 2)* (1931).

- There is now no absolute right to insist on non-disclosure upon the ground of the immunity. Whatever be the ground of the objection, it is conditional and depends upon the decision of the court: see *Sankey v Whitlam* (1978).

- Only rarely can documents relating to the industrial or commercial activities of government come within the immunity, especially in time of peace: see *Robinson* (1931); *Harbour Corporation of Queensland v Vessey Chemicals Pty Ltd* (1986); *Hooker Corporation Ltd v Darling Harbour Authority* (1987).

- The mere fact that the production of a document might prejudice the Crown's case is not a justification for non-disclosure: see *Robinson*. However, the fact that disclosure may dry up a source of information is of some significance: see *Rogers v Home Secretary* (1973); *D's* case (1978); *Cochrane v Byron Shire Council* (1992); *AG (NSW) v Stuart* (1994); cf *Woollahra Municipal Council v Westpac Banking Corporation* (1994).

- The court:
  - ○ is entitled to require, and should require, a certificate or an affidavit from the responsible minister (or some other proper officer) supporting any claim for non-disclosure; and
  - ○ reserves the right to inspect the documents in question (even *in camera*: see *Alister v R* (1983)) and to rule on the claim.

- The certificate or affidavit supporting the claim is no longer conclusive: see *Conway v Rimmer* (1968); *Sankey v Whitlam* (1978); cf *Duncan v Cammell Laird & Co Ltd* (1942).

The making of a claim

It has been held that public interest immunity is not dependent on a claim being made by one of the parties and that the court should claim the immunity if the point is not taken by the parties: see *Duncan*. However, this is now doubted.

Two different types of claim can be made:

- A 'contents' claim, where the contents of the documents are such that objection can be made in the public interest to their disclosure.

- A 'class' claim, where the documents fall within a 'class' of documents (for example, cabinet documents) which ought, in the public interest, to be withheld: see *Duncan*; *Commonwealth v Northern Land Council* (1993).

Public interest immunity may only properly be claimed where disclosure of the documents would do *present* damage to the public interest.

Examples of material in relation to which public interest immunity is commonly claimed include:

- confidential cabinet deliberations and discussions: see *Northern Land Council*;
- material prejudicial to national security: see *Duncan*; *Alister*;
- the identity of police informers: see *D's* case; *Cain v Glass (No 2)* (1985); *Stuart*;
- information prejudicial to ongoing investigations: see *Hilton v Wells* (1985); *Cochrane*; *Stuart*.

Merely confidential material, the release of which would not be contrary to the public interest, may not be properly claimed under public interest immunity: see *Alfred Crompton Amusement Machines Ltd v Customs and Excise Commissioner (No 2)* (1974); *Kanthal v Minister for Industry Technology and Commerce* (1987).

The role of the court

It is for the court to decide whether or not a claim for public interest immunity should prevail.

Documents may be withheld from disclosure only if and to the extent that the public interest renders it necessary: see *Sankey*.

In reaching its decision on a claim for non-disclosure of certain documents, the court is to balance two competing factors (see *Conway*; *Sankey*):

1   The public interest that requires certain matters to remain secret (for example, on the ground of national security, or to avoid serious damage to the proper working of government).

    According to this factor, 'it is inherent in the nature of things that government at a high level cannot function without some degree of secrecy': see *Sankey, per* Gibbs ACJ.

2   The public interest that requires that, in the administration of justice, all relevant evidence should be available to the court.

According to this factor, 'the very integrity of the judicial system and public confidence in the system depend on full disclosure of the facts': see *US v Nixon* (1978).

No documents are absolutely inaccessible, whether the objection to their disclosure be in the form of a 'contents' or 'class' claim.

However, in the case of certain types of 'class' documents (for example, cabinet documents):

- strong considerations of public policy militate against disclosure (particularly in civil proceedings);
- the court will lean initially against disclosure; and
- it requires exceptional circumstances for those considerations to be outweighed by the public interest in the due administration of justice: see *Northern Land Council*.

The decision of the court

The court:

- may refuse to conduct an *in camera* inspection of documents unless the party seeking access to them can show that it is 'on the cards', 'likely', 'very likely' or even 'reasonably probable' that they will assist their case: see *Burmah Oil Co Ltd v Bank of England* (1980); *Air Canada v Secretary of State for Trade* (1983); *Alister*;
- will ordinarily refuse, in the case of cabinet documents, to order production of the documents to the court unless there are 'quite exceptional circumstances' giving rise to a 'significant likelihood' that the public interest in the administration of justice outweighs the public interest in confidentiality: see *Northern Land Council*;
- may restrict, even where it has ordered production of documents, access to them, for example, provide them only to the applicant's lawyers, perhaps on their undertaking not to divulge the contents to anyone, even their own client: see *Kanthal*.

Powers of the legislature

In *Egan v Chadwick* (1999), the NSW Court of Appeal held that the NSW Legislative Council had the power to require the production of documents held by the executive arm of government, even documents in respect of which claims of legal professional privilege and public interest immunity had been or could be made, to the extent to which access to any such documents was 'reasonably necessary' for the exercise by the Legislative Council of its functions.

As regards documents the subject of a claim in respect of public interest immunity, the court held that the performance of the legislative and accountability functions of the Legislative Council may well require access to information the disclosure of which, on balance, may not be in the public interest. However, access to such documents may still be 'reasonably necessary' for the performance of the Legislative Council's functions.

The court nevertheless held that the power to call for the production of documents should, at least, be restricted to documents that do not, directly or indirectly, reveal the deliberations of Cabinet. To compel the production of documents that would reveal the deliberations of Cabinet would, it was held, be inconsistent with the doctrine of collective ministerial responsibility.

However, the revelation of other documents, including documents prepared outside Cabinet (for example, in the public service) for submission to Cabinet – which, in a court of law, would ordinarily still attract a successful claim of public interest – *may not*, depending on their content, be inconsistent with the doctrine of collective ministerial responsibility.

8 The Administrative Decisions (Judicial Review) Act

You should be familiar with the following areas:

- the concept of a 'decision to which [the] Act applies'
- the meaning of the words 'administrative character'
- the meaning of the expression 'under an enactment'
- what constitutes 'conduct engaged in for the purpose of making a decision'
- the statutory test of legal standing
- the various grounds for review of decisions and conduct (and differences from the common law)

Introduction

The Administrative Decisions (Judicial Review) Act 1977 (Cth) ('the ADJR Act 1977') was assented to on 16 June 1977 and commenced on 1 October 1980.

The ADJR Act 1977 is, in many respects, a codification of the common law mechanisms for judicial review of decisions made pursuant to *Commonwealth* enactments. (See definition of 'enactment' in s 3(1): 'enactment' includes most *Commonwealth* statutes and statutory rules.)

However, the grounds for review of Commonwealth administrative action:

- differ in some respects from those of the common law; and
- may also be invoked in relation to 'conduct engaged in for the purpose of making a decision' otherwise reviewable under the legislation.

Jurisdiction

The Federal Court of Australia has jurisdiction to hear and determine applications for review made to it under the ADJR Act 1977: see s 8.

The court's role under the ADJR Act 1977 is one of 'judicial review' of the lawfulness of a decision and not its merits: see s 16.

The court, when reviewing decisions in the exercise of its jurisdiction under the ADJR Act 1977:

- can disregard privative clauses in force at the commencement of the ADJR Act 1977: see s 4; and
- may, in its discretion, decline relief having regard to, among other things, the availability of alternative remedies and causes of action: see s 10(2).

Judicial review under the ADJR Act 1977

The ADJR Act 1977 makes provision for judicial review of:

- a 'decision to which [the] Act applies', other than:
  - ○ a decision by the Governor General; or
  - ○ a decision included in any of the classes of decisions set out in Schedule 1 to the ADJR Act 1977; and
- 'conduct engaged in for the purpose of making a decision' otherwise reviewable under the ADJR Act 1977.

Decisions to which the ADJR Act 1977 applies

For a decision to be reviewable under the ADJR Act 1977, it must be a 'decision to which this Act applies': see s 3(1).

The necessary elements are as follows:

- there must be a 'decision';
- the decision must be 'of an administrative character';
- the decision must be one made 'under an enactment';
- the decision must not otherwise be excluded from review under the ADJR Act 1977 (see above).

'Decision'

The word 'decision' is not itself defined in the ADJR Act 1977. However, see:

- the interpretation of 'making a decision' in s 3(2); and
- the interpretation of a 'deemed decision' in s 3(8).

The making of a 'report' or 'recommendation' *before* a reviewable decision is made is *itself* taken, for the purposes of the ADJR Act 1977, to be the making of a decision (but *only* where provision is made by an enactment for the making of such a report or recommendation): see s 3(3).

A report or recommendation made otherwise than as a statutory condition precedent to the making of a reviewable decision, or in the ordinary course of general administrative processes, is not taken to be a decision for the purposes of the ADJR Act 1977: see *Gourgaud v Lawton* (1982); *Ross v Costigan* (1982).

'Administrative character'

The phrase 'decision of an administrative character':

- is incapable of precise definition;
- must not be interpreted or applied rigidly but should be given a wide interpretation;
- looks to the 'nature' and 'character' of the decision itself rather than to the person or body making the decision;
- excludes decisions of a non-administrative, 'different' character such as legislative, judicial and perhaps ministerial, as well as certain administrative decisions more of a legislative, rather than administrative, character: see *Botany Bay City Council v Minister for Transport and Regional Development* (1996);
- includes:
  - the application of a general policy or rule to a particular case; and
  - the making of an individual decision.

See, generally, *Hamblin v Duffy* (1981) and *Tooheys Ltd v Minister for Business and Consumer Affairs* (1981).

Case example

> A magistrate, after conducting an inquiry under s 12(1) and (2) of
> the Marriage Act 1961 (Cth), decided to dismiss an application for
> an order authorising a 16 year old woman to marry. Moore J in the
> Federal Court held that the decision, although made by a
> magistrate, was 'of an administrative character' which could be
> reviewed under the ADJR Act 1977.
>
> *K v Cullen* (1994)

'Under an enactment'

For a decision to be made 'under an enactment', it is not necessary that
the particular decision making power be precisely stated.

In each case, the question to be asked is one of substance, that is,
whether, in effect, the decision is made 'under an enactment' or
otherwise: see *Burns v Australian National University* (1982), *per*
Ellicott J.

Case example

> The appointment of a university professor was terminated, and
> the person in question sought to invoke the ADJR Act in respect of
> the decision. It was held that the salient decision was made
> pursuant to a contract of employment and not 'under an
> enactment', even though the ultimate power to appoint and
> employ staff was a statutory one.
>
> *Australian National University v Burns* (1982)

Problems of interpretation can, however, arise where the decision:

- is an essential step towards the making of a reviewable decision;
  but
- is not the decision actually required by the enactment.

For a decision to be reviewable under the ADJR Act 1977, it must:

- be a 'substantive' determination; and
- generally, but not always, entail a decision which is 'final' or
  'operative' or 'determinative', at least in a practical sense, of the
  issue of fact falling for consideration: see *Australian Broadcasting
  Tribunal v Bond* (1990).

The test is *not* whether a particular decision is simply a logical
precondition for the making of the ultimate or operative decision, but
whether the decision is one for which provision is made by or under a
statute: see *Bond*.

A decision made (for example, conclusion reached, finding or ruling made) 'along the way' in the course of reasoning leading to the making of an ultimate reviewable decision is ordinarily unreviewable under the ADJR Act. However, where the statute provides for the making of a finding or ruling on that particular point, so that the decision, though an 'intermediate' decision, can accurately be described as a decision 'under an enactment', the position will be different, and the finding or ruling will be reviewable: see *Bond*; cf *Lamb v Moss* (1983).

Case example

> The Australian Broadcasting Tribunal conducted a hearing into the question of whether the respondent companies' commercial broadcasting licences under the Broadcasting Act 1942 (Cth) should be renewed. The Tribunal found that the first respondent had been guilty of improper conduct in various respects and concluded that he would not be found to be a fit and proper person to hold a licence under that Act. The Tribunal further found that, by reason of the first respondent's control of the licensee companies, they were no longer fit and proper persons to hold the licences. The High Court held that the finding that the licensees were no longer fit and proper persons to hold their licences was a decision reviewable under the ADJR Act 1977. However, the finding that the first respondent would not be found to be a fit and proper person to hold a licence was not a decision within the ADJR Act 1977, since the Broadcasting Act made no provision for the making of a finding or ruling on that point.
>
> *Australian Broadcasting Tribunal v Bond and Others* (1990)

Conduct engaged in for the purpose of making a decision

For 'conduct' to be reviewable under the ADJR Act 1977, it must:

- be part of a decision making process leading to the making of a decision to which the ADJR Act 1977 otherwise applies: see *Gourgaud v Lawton* (1982);
- involve something which is 'procedural', and not 'substantive', in nature: see *Australian Broadcasting Tribunal v Bond and Others* (1990);
- point to action taken, rather than a decision made, for the purpose of making a reviewable decision: see *Bond*.

Mere thought processes do not amount to 'conduct': see *Ricegrowers Co-operative Mills Ltd v Bannerman* (1981).

Conduct engaged in for the purpose of making a decision will include the 'doing of any act preparatory to the making of the decision', for example, the taking of evidence or the holding of an inquiry or investigation: see s 3(5).

Substantive decisions, findings of fact and inferences drawn from findings of fact are generally unreviewable as conduct, unless what is alleged is some breach of a 'procedural' requirement in the course of the conduct involved in reaching the relevant conclusion.

Grounds for review

The ADJR Act 1977 largely codifies the common law grounds of judicial review (although there are some important differences which are discussed below): see ss 5 ('decision') and 6 ('conduct'). (See also s 7, which is, in effect, a statutory alternative to mandamus.)

The grounds of review are as follows:

- breach of the 'rules of natural justice': see ss 5(1)(a), 6(1)(a);
- procedural *ultra vires*: see ss 5(1)(b), 6(1)(b);
- no jurisdiction: see ss 5(1)(c), 6(1)(c);
- substantive *ultra vires*: see ss 5(1)(d), 6(1)(d);
- 'improper exercise of power' (that is, relevant/irrelevant considerations, improper purpose, bad faith, acting under dictation, acting on a policy, manifest unreasonableness, uncertainty, or otherwise an 'abuse of power'): see ss 5(1)(e), 5(2), 6(1)(e), 6(2);
- error of law ('whether or not the error appears on the face of the record'): see ss 5(1)(f), 6(1)(f);
- fraud: see ss 5(1)(g), 6(1)(g);
- 'no evidence': see ss 5(1)(h), 6(1)(h);
- 'otherwise contrary to law': see ss 5(1)(j), 6(1)(j).

Natural justice

As to breach of the rules of natural justice (procedural fairness), the ground does not extend to all decisions, but only those to which the rules would otherwise apply at common law: see *Capello v Minister for Immigration and Ethnic Affairs* (1980).

Procedural *ultra vires*

This ground of review is only made out where a designated procedure is required to be followed.

No jurisdiction

This ground of review includes, at the very least, the common law ground of lack (or want) of jurisdiction.

Excess of jurisdiction:

- in the traditional sense, is arguably also included within this ground, but may also fall within other stated grounds (for example, procedural *ultra vires*, error of law);
- in its broad or extended sense: see *Anisminic Ltd v Foreign Compensation Commission* (1969), may not be included within this ground, but will come within either or both of the 'improper exercise of power' and 'error of law' grounds.

Improper exercise of power

The 'acting under dictation' ground ('at the direction or behest of another person') may be narrower than the common law, where dictation can occur even though the other person or body gives no direction that a particular approach should be followed: see *Evans v Donaldson* (1909).

The 'abuse of power' ground:

- is presumably intended as a general catch-all ground;
- would permit the court to develop new grounds of review;
- will also presumably include the not otherwise expressly stated common law ground of 'fettering discretion'.

A fact-finding error involving unsound reasoning, or the drawing of faulty inferences, may be reviewable as an 'improper exercise' of power if it is:

- otherwise reviewable as a 'decision'; and
- 'manifestly unreasonable' or arbitrary (for example, where there is an absence of a legally defensible foundation in the factual material or illogicality): see *Minister for Immigration and Ethnic Affairs v Teo* (1995).

Error of law

The 'error of law' ground allows judicial review for both:

- jurisdictional error of law; and
- non-jurisdictional error of law,

whether or not the error appears on the face of the record of the decision. Thus, the concept of 'extended jurisdictional error' (see *Anisminic*) has been accepted for the purposes of the ADJR Act 1977.

The 'error of law' ground, read in conjunction with:

- the 'improper exercise of power' ground; or
- the 'no evidence' ground,

or both, will permit resort to the ADJR Act 1977 in certain circumstances where a decision perceived to be 'incorrect' or 'wrong' could not otherwise be successfully challenged on an 'error of law' basis pursuant to some statutory right of appeal on a question of law (for example, where there has been a serious error in fact-finding).

Fraud

This ground of review appears to merely reproduce the common law.

No evidence

The stated 'no evidence' ground, in itself, is narrower than the common law rule. It is not to be taken to be made out unless one of two situations exists:

- non-existence of an essential fact;
- reliance on a non-existent fact: see ss 5(3) and 6(3).

The view has been expressed that:

- the 'error of law' ground of review, with or without the 'improper exercise of power' ground, embrace the common law 'no evidence' ground as it was accepted and applied before the commencement of the ADJR Act 1977: see *Bond* (1990), *per* Mason CJ; *Szelagowicz v Stocker* (1994), *per* Davies and Einfeld JJ; and
- the stated 'no evidence' ground of review merely expands that ground of review: see *Bond* (1990), *per* Mason CJ; cf *Szelagowicz*, *per* Davies and Einfeld JJ.

An error in fact-finding, if a 'decision' to which the ADJR Act 1977 applies, will also be reviewable on the ground that there is no probative evidence to support it, and an inference will be reviewable on the ground that it was not reasonably open on the facts: see *Minister for Immigration and Ethnic Affairs v Teo* (1995).

Otherwise contrary to law

This ground of review is also presumably intended as a general catch-all ground.

Standing

A 'person aggrieved' by a decision to which the ADJR Act 1977 applies may make application to the Federal Court for review of that decision.
   The test of standing:

- is not to be given a narrow construction; and
- is not confined to persons who can establish that they have a legal interest at stake in the making of the decision: see *Tooheys Ltd v Minister for Business and Consumer Affairs* (1981).

A 'person aggrieved' includes a person who can show a grievance which will be suffered as a result of the decision beyond which that person has as an ordinary member of the public: see *Tooheys*; *Right to Life Association (NSW) v Secretary, Department of Human Services and Health (Cth)* (1995).

Case example

An incorporated association had as its object opposition to abortion. Statutory permission had been granted by the respondent for the importation for clinical testing of abortifacients. The appellant association sought judicial review of a 'decision' not to cancel the permission. The Full Federal Court held that the association was not a 'person aggrieved' within the meaning of the ADJR Act 1977 as its interest was no more than that of any other member of the community. The court also held that there was no 'decision' for the purposes of the ADJR Act 1977 as the respondent was not under a duty to act on the request of the association.

Right to Life Association (NSW) v Secretary,
Department of Human Services and Health (Cth) (1995)

Reasons for decision

A person entitled to apply for review under the ADJR Act 1977 has a right to obtain a statement of reasons for the decision (except in respect of certain excluded decisions): see s 13.

The statement must also:

*   include findings on material questions of fact; and
*   refer to the evidence or other material on which those findings were based: see s 13(1).

A full and further statement of reasons can be obtained if the statement originally provided is inadequate: see s 13(7).

9 The Administrative Appeals Tribunal

You should be familiar with the following areas:

• the nature of administrative review 'on the merits'
• the jurisdiction of the Administrative Appeals Tribunal (Cth)
• what constitutes a 'decision' for the purposes of the legislation
• the powers of the Tribunal
• the meaning of the expression 'person whose interests are affected'
• the practice of the Tribunal in relation to lawful ministerial policy

Introduction

The Administrative Appeals Tribunal Act 1975 (Cth) ('the AAT Act 1975') was assented to on 28 August 1975 and commenced on 1 July 1976.

The AAT Act 1975 makes provision for the administrative (as opposed to 'judicial') review of 'decisions' made in the exercise of powers that have been conferred by an Act of the Parliament of the *Commonwealth*.

The Administrative Appeals Tribunal ('the Tribunal'), set up by the AAT Act 1975, is a special administrative tribunal concerned with reviewing, 'on the merits', decisions reviewable under the Act.

Some Australian States (for example, New South Wales, Victoria) have set up their own Administrative Appeals Tribunals or similar bodies; see, for example, Administrative Decisions Tribunal Act 1997 (NSW); Administrative Law Act 1978 (Vic).

Legal status and jurisdiction of the Tribunal

Legal status

The Tribunal:

- is an administrative body with limited authority; and
- is not vested with the judicial power of the Commonwealth: see *Re Adams and Tax Agents' Board* (1976).

Jurisdiction

Not all decisions made by federal government agencies are reviewable by the Tribunal. The jurisdiction of the Tribunal is now conferred by express provision in an Act of the Parliament of the Commonwealth: see s 25(1).

Meaning of 'decision'

There is a broad definition of 'decision' in s 3(3) of the AAT Act 1975. The expression 'decision' for the purposes of the Act:

- refers not only to a decision made but also to action taken to implement it;
- includes a purported decision: see *Collector of Customs v Brian Lawlor Automotive Pty Ltd* (1979) and an invalid decision: see *Re Baran and Secretary, Department of Primary Industries and Energy* (1988).

Role and functions of the Tribunal

The role of the Tribunal is to review a reviewable decision 'on the merits'.

In that regard, the Tribunal:

- is not restricted to considerations which are relevant to judicial determinations;
- is empowered to decide whether a particular decision is 'the correct and preferable one on the material before the tribunal': see *Drake v Minister for Immigration and Ethnic Affairs* (1979);

- is also empowered to review the findings of fact and policies upon which the original decision was based;
- must make its own independent assessment and determination of the particular matter before it: see *Drake*;
- has authority over the matter before it equal to that of the original decision maker: see s 43;
- must act 'judicially', that is, with 'judicial fairness and detachment': see *Drake*.

Insofar as government policy is concerned, the Tribunal:

- may take such policy into account but is not bound to determine the matter before it according to government or ministerial policy unless so required by statute: see *Drake*;
- adopts a practice of applying lawful ministerial policy, 'unless there are cogent reasons to the contrary': see *Re Drake v Minister for Immigration and Ethnic Affairs (No 2)* (1979).

In some jurisdictions (for example, New South Wales), the Tribunal, in determining an application for review of a reviewable decision, MUST give effect to any relevant government policy in force at the time the reviewable decision was made, except to the extent that the policy:

- is contrary to law; or
- produces an unjust decision in the circumstances of the case.

Case example

A citizen of the United States of America was ordered to be deported from Australia after he had been convicted of an offence. The Tribunal affirmed the decision of the Minister, but an appeal against the order was allowed by the Federal Court and the matter was remitted to the Tribunal for rehearing. It was found by the Federal Court that the Tribunal, in placing too much weight on the Minister's policy statement with respect to deportation, had failed, in the circumstances of the case, to make its own independent assessment and determination of the particular matter. The Court emphasised the fact that the Tribunal was set up as an independent administrative authority charged with the responsibility of arriving at the 'correct and preferable' decision on the material before it. On rehearing, the Tribunal stated that whilst it was not bound by lawful ministerial policy, it ought to adopt a general practice of applying such policy unless there were cogent reasons to the contrary. If, for example, it were shown that the application of the policy would work an injustice in a particular case, a cogent reason would then be shown.

Drake v Minister for Immigration and Ethnic Affairs (1979);
Re Drake v Minister for Immigration and Ethnic Affairs (No 2) (1979)

See also *Re Becker and Minister for Immigration and Ethnic Affairs* (1977) as to the application of government policy.

In that case, it was stated that the Tribunal would ask itself the following four questions:

1   Is this a case where the decision maker has power to act?
2   If there is a policy purporting to govern the exercise of the discretion, is that policy consistent with the relevant legislation?
3   If there is such a policy, is any cause shown why that policy ought not to apply, either generally or in this particular case?
4   On the material before the Tribunal, and having regard to any policy considerations deemed relevant, was the original decision the 'correct and preferable' one?

Applications for review

Persons who may apply for review

A 'person ... whose interests are affected' by a decision reviewable under the AAT Act 1975 may make application to the Tribunal for review of the decision: see s 27(1).

The relevant 'interests':

•   need not be pecuniary or even specific legal rights; but
•   *must* (as opposed to *may*) be 'immediately and directly affected' by the decision under review: see *Re McHattan and Collector of Customs (NSW)* (1977).

It may be that a person whose interests are affected need not be present in Australia: see *Re Mere Akuhata-Brown and Minister for Immigration and Ethnic Affairs* (1981).

Statement of reasons

The original decision maker must furnish a statement of reasons:

- if asked to do so by a person whose interests are affected: see s 28; and
- in any event, within 28 days after receiving notice of the application for review: see s 37.

The statement must also:

- include findings on material questions of fact; and
- refer to the evidence or other material on which those findings were based: see s 28(1).

The Tribunal may make an order requiring the original decision maker to provide a further statement containing 'better particulars': see s 38. The statement:

- must be a factual account of what occurred;
- must not be vague or general; and
- must be complete and in intelligible language: see *Re Palmer and Minister for the Capital Territory* (1978).

Lodgement of application

An application for review under the AAT Act 1975 must be lodged within 28 days of receiving:

- notification of the decision if reasons are provided with it; or
- a formal statement of reasons if requested under the AAT Act 1975: see s 29(2).

Consideration and determination of applications

Procedure

The Tribunal's procedure is, subject to the AAT Act 1975, within the discretion of the Tribunal: see s 33(1)(a). In practice, the Tribunal relies on:

- oral argument; and
- agreed statements of facts and written submissions.

Proceedings are to be conducted 'with as little formality and technicality', and 'with as much expedition', as possible: see s 33(1)(b).

The rules of procedural fairness nevertheless apply to proceedings of the Tribunal: see *Australian Postal Commission v Hayes* (1989); *Marelic v Comcare* (1993).

However, an applicant is clearly not entitled to all of the procedural safeguards of a trial: see *Marelic* (in which it was stated that the rule in *Browne v Dunn* (1894) applied with qualification in proceedings of the Tribunal).

An applicant may be represented before the AAT Act 1975 by a lawyer or any other person: see s 32.

The Tribunal:

* has wide powers to call for government documents: see ss 37, 38; and

* may release information to the parties (despite a certificate by the Attorney General that disclosure would be contrary to the public interest) if it is desirable in the interest of securing the effective performance of the Tribunal's functions: see s 36(4).

There is provision for preliminary conferences (aimed at conciliation), which are normally held in private: see s 34.

Hearings are normally held in public, although the Tribunal has a discretion to direct that a hearing or part of a hearing shall take place in private: see s 35(1).

Decision making powers of the Tribunal

The Tribunal may (except to the extent otherwise provided in an enactment) affirm, vary or set aside the decision under review. Where it sets aside the decision, the Tribunal may:

* make a decision in substitution for the original decision; or

* remit the matter for reconsideration in accordance with any directions or recommendations of the Tribunal: see s 43(1).

Reasons for decisions

The reasons for the Tribunal's decision must be given: see s 43(2). The reasons do not have to comply with a standard of perfection: see *Bisley Investment Corporation Ltd v Australian Broadcasting Tribunal* (1982), but must nevertheless:

* include the Tribunal's findings on material questions of fact and refer to the evidence; and

- refer to the evidence or other material on which those findings were based: see s 43(2B); see *Blackwood Hodge (Australia) Pty Ltd v Collector of Customs (NSW)* (1980).

Appeals from the Tribunal

There is a right of appeal to the Federal Court of Australia on a question of law: see s 44(1).

The Tribunal itself may refer a question of law to the Federal Court: see ss 44 and 45.

NOTE: The Federal Government proposes a major restructure of its administrative tribunal system involving, among other things, the creation of a new Administrative Review Tribunal, which would replace the Administrative Appeals Tribunal and various other tribunals. At the time of publication, the legislation has not been enacted.

10 The Ombudsman

You should be familiar with the following areas:

- the role and functions of an ombudsman
- the meaning of 'matter of administration'
- the meaning of 'wrong conduct'

Introduction

An ombudsman is an independent person appointed to investigate complaints made to him or her about action or inaction:

- that relate to a 'matter of administration';
- taken by a government department or other public authority (or any officer or employee of the department or authority).

The office of ombudsman is of Swedish origin, having been created there in 1809.

The word 'ombudsman' means 'representative' or 'agent'. However, an ombudsman is:

- certainly not the representative or agent of the authority the subject of the complaint; and
- arguably not a representative or agent of the complainant.

An ombudsman combines:

- the judicial functions of a magistrate or judge; and
- the administrative functions of an inquisitor.

The federal ombudsman legislation is the Ombudsman Act 1976. The Australian States also passed similar legislation in the 1970s: see Parliamentary Commissioner Act 1971 (WA); Ombudsman Act 1974 (NSW).

Ombudsmen in most jurisdictions also have certain functions to perform in relation to freedom of information legislation (see Chapter 11).

Jurisdiction

An ombudsman is ordinarily empowered to investigate:

- action or inaction; or
- alleged action or inaction,

that 'relates to' a 'matter of administration'.

'Matter of administration'

The question of what constitutes a 'matter of administration' is quite complicated.

Most ombudsmen adopt a fairly broad view of the meaning of the words, consistent with several Australian and overseas judicial decisions: see *Glenister v Dillon* (1976); *Glenister v Dillon (No 2)* (1977); *Re Ombudsman of Ontario and Health Disciplines Board of Ontario* (1979).

'Matters of administration':

- will include a wide range of governmental activity carried on by bodies other than the legislature and the judiciary, that is, the performance of executive or administrative functions;
- arguably do not include 'policy' considerations, where the matter in question involves policy and not simply administration: see *Salisbury City Council v Biganovsky* (1990).

The inclusion of the words 'relates to' means that an ombudsman:

- is not restricted to investigating a 'matter of administration' strictly so called; and
- may also investigate any other action which might be regarded as reasonably incidental to the performance of executive or administrative functions: see *Glenister v Dillon* (1976).

Excluded conduct

Each piece of ombudsman legislation excludes certain matters from the ombudsman's jurisdiction, for example, actions by a minister, magistrate or judge and actions of government authorities specifically excluded by the applicable legislation.

Investigations

An ombudsman may investigate a matter within jurisdiction:

- on his or her own motion;
- upon receipt of a written complaint by any person; or
- upon request by the legislature.

Relief by way of mandamus will not lie to compel the ombudsman to investigate a complaint. The ombudsman has a discretion whether or not to investigate: see *Re Fletcher's Application* (1970).

The ombudsman has a discretion to decline to investigate a complaint in certain circumstances (for example, where the complaint is frivolous or vexatious). In the exercise of that discretion, the ombudsman will have regard to, and (in some jurisdictions) may even be constrained by, the existence of alternative remedies and avenues of review and appeal available to the complainant.

The investigation may be conducted in such manner as the ombudsman thinks fit, subject to compliance with procedural and other requirements set out in the legislation.

Procedural fairness (in particular, the right to be heard) applies, but it is arguable that it only applies to the extent provided for in the relevant legislation: see s 8(5) of the Ombudsman Act 1976 (Cth). See also *R v Dixon ex p Prince and Oliver* (1979).

Under the Ombudsman Act 1974 (NSW), the ombudsman is relevantly required to:

- give notice to the public authority (including a person) the subject of investigation, describing the conduct to be the subject of investigation (see s 16); and
- inform the authority (or person), where the ombudsman considers there are grounds for adverse comment in respect of the authority or person, as to the substance of the grounds of the adverse comment, and to give the authority or person an opportunity to make submissions: see s 24(2).

Section 24(1)(a) of the Ombudsman Act 1974 provides that, in an investigation under the Act, the ombudsman shall 'if practicable' (that is, reasonably practicable, having regard, among other things, to the circumstances of the particular case and to what is 'capable of being done or accomplished with the available resources whatever they may be': see *Potter v Neave* (1944), *per* Mayo J) give the public authority, whose conduct is the subject of investigation, an opportunity to make submissions on the conduct.

Even though the statute may be read as leaving the choice of courses at large to the ombudsman (as regards an opportunity to be heard), it should ordinarily be interpreted and understood as meaning that *prima facie* the course which would deny such an opportunity should be followed 'only in exceptional or special cases': see *Commissioner of Police v Tanos* (1958), *per* Dixon CJ and Webb J. The fact that the legislation contains some provisions commensurate with some of the rules of procedural fairness does not necessarily exclude or displace a wider application of those rules in a particular context: see *Annetts v McCann* (1990); cf *Valley Watch Inc v Minister for Planning* (1994).

The ombudsman's powers, including powers of compulsion, are limited to those necessary to enable the proper investigation of complaints of wrong conduct.

'Wrong conduct'

An ombudsman is required to determine whether the action or inaction complained of constitutes 'wrong conduct': see s 15(1) of the Ombudsman Act 1976 (Cth) and s 26 of the Ombudsman Act 1974 (NSW).

'Wrong conduct' includes such things as:

- conduct which appears to have been contrary to law;
- conduct that was unreasonable, unjust, oppressive or improperly discriminatory;
- conduct that was based on a law or practice which is or may be unreasonable, unjust, oppressive or improperly discriminatory;
- conduct for which reasons should have been given but are not given; and
- conduct that was 'otherwise wrong'.

The ombudsman:

- cannot substitute his or her own decision for that of the decision maker;
- may not question the merits of an administrative decision in the absence of any element of maladministration;
- must inform the complainant of the outcome of the investigation;
- will ordinarily only make a report (which may or may not be made available to the complainant) where:
  - ɔ the matter has been formally investigated; and
  - ɔ the ombudsman's findings are critical of the public authority.

11 Freedom of Information Legislation

You should be familiar with the following areas:

- the various methods by which freedom of information legislation is intended to extend as far as possible the right to access to information
- the making of an application for access to documents held by an agency
- the making of an application for amendment of an agency's records
- the more important classes of exempt documents (for example, cabinet documents, internal working documents)
- review and appeal rights

Introduction

The United States of America passed freedom of information ('FOI') legislation in 1966. That legislation has served as a model for much of the Australian FOI legislation in particular, the Freedom of Information Act 1982 (Cth).

Australia was the first country with a Westminster-style government to introduce FOI legislation at the national level.

The FOI statutes of the Australian States and Territories are largely modelled on the federal legislation.

Object of FOI legislation

The primary stated object of FOI legislation is to extend, as far as possible, the right of members of the public to access information in the possession of government agencies: see s 3 of the FOI Act 1982 (Cth). This is accomplished by:

- requiring government agencies to make publicly available certain information about their functions, operations and the types of documents in their possession; and

- conferring upon a member of the public a legally enforceable right of access to documents (other than so called 'exempt documents') in the possession of a government agency.

Another object of FOI legislation is to make provision for the amendment or notation of personal records where a member of the public claims that a document held by an agency is incomplete, incorrect, out of date or misleading.

FOI legislation is not intended to prevent or discourage the 'informal' publication of information, the giving of access to documents or the amendment of records as permitted or required by or under any other Act or law.

Thus, where an agency has an existing policy of providing informal access to certain documents, reliance on those arrangements can continue, without the need for a formal application under the FOI legislation (unless it is necessary or desirable).

Applications for access to an agency's documents

Each FOI Act contains requirements with respect to the making of an application for access to an agency's documents.

For example, s 17 of the Freedom of Information Act 1989 (NSW) provides that an application for access:

- must be in writing;
- must specify that it is made under the FOI Act;
- must be accompanied by the required application fee;
- must contain such information as is reasonably necessary to enable the document to be identified;
- must specify an address in Australia to which notices under the Act should be sent;
- must be lodged at an office of the agency.

The application may request that access to the document be given in a particular form (for example, a reasonable opportunity to inspect the document, receiving a copy of the document, etc).

Exempt documents

An agency *may*, but need not necessarily, refuse access to a document in its possession if it is an 'exempt document'. (However, see 'Reverse FOI', below.)

The classes of exempt documents are set out in the applicable FOI legislation.

Some of the more important classes of exempt documents are discussed below.

Documents affecting 'personal affairs' and documents affecting 'business affairs'

A document is an exempt document if it contains matter the disclosure of which would involve the unreasonable disclosure of information concerning:

- the 'personal affairs' of any other person (whether living or dead); or
- the 'business affairs' of any other person.

'Personal affairs' encompass any matters of private concern to an individual: see *Re Resch and Department of Veterans' Affairs* (1986).

As to 'business affairs', see *Re Actors' Equity Association of Australia and Australian Broadcasting Tribunal (No 2)* (1984).

'Cabinet documents' and 'Executive Council documents'

Documents (including preliminary drafts) prepared for submission to Cabinet or the Executive Council, whether or not so submitted, are exempt, as are the official records of those bodies.

The exemptions include any documents which would disclose any deliberation or decision of the body in question.

A document is not exempt simply because it was before the body in question when it made its decision: see *Re Rae and Department of Prime Minister and Cabinet* (1986). It is not to be concluded that there was deliberation in respect of matter contained in a document merely because it was before the body at a meeting of the body: see *Rae*.

'Internal working documents'

A document is only exempt under this category if it is one:

- which relates to the deliberative processes or decision making functions of the agency; and
- the disclosure of which would disclose any opinion, advice or recommendation or consultation or deliberation obtained, etc in the course of those processes or functions; and
- the disclosure of which would, on balance, be contrary to the public interest.

The FOI Act 1982 (Cth) uses the phrase 'deliberative processes' which has been interpreted as meaning 'thinking processes': see *Re James and Australian National University* (1984); *Re Fewster and Department of Prime Minister and Cabinet* (1986).

The exemption does not apply to 'purely factual material'.

The document in question must:

- have an 'administrative' purpose; and
- be actually part of the decision making process (which would exclude the actual making of the decision and subsequent steps to implement the decision).

A document may be exempt under this class even if it originated outside the agency: see *Harris v Australian Broadcasting Corporation* (1984).

As to whether disclosure would be in the 'public interest', this essentially involves the weighing, in the particular case, of the benefits or advantages to the public in granting disclosure against any possible adverse effects or disadvantages in so doing (including whether disclosure would be likely to impede or have an adverse effect upon the efficient administration of the agency concerned): see *Re James and Australian National University* (1984).

There are a number of factors relevant, or potentially relevant, to the 'public interest' question, including:

- the age of the documents;
- the importance of the issues discussed;
- the continuing relevance of those issues in relation to matters still under consideration;
- the extent to which premature disclosure may reveal sensitive information that may be misunderstood or misapplied;
- the extent to which the subject matter of the documents is already within the public knowledge;

- the need to preserve confidentiality having regard to the subject matter of the communication and the circumstances in which it was made.

(See *Re Lianos and Secretary, Department of Social Security* (1985).)

'Documents subject to legal professional privilege'

'Legal professional privilege' extends to all communications and documents brought into existence for the purpose of the obtaining or giving of legal advice in all matters in which a legal practitioner is engaged in a professional capacity (and not merely in relation to litigation).

The essential question is whether the 'dominant purpose' (see ss 118–20 of the Evidence Act 1995 (Cth)) for which the document was brought into existence was for either seeking or giving legal advice or for use in existing or anticipated litigation. (Formerly, the 'sole purpose' test was applied in Australia: see *Waterford v Commonwealth of Australia* (1987).)

If that test is satisfied, it is immaterial whether the document also contains 'factual' or 'administrative' material: see *Re Ralkon Agricultural Company Pty Ltd and Aboriginal Development Commission* (1986).

The privilege will extend to a legally qualified employee acting in the capacity of an 'independent' legal adviser (*Waterford*), but not where the person merely provides advice on matters of policy or administrative arrangement: *Re Lawless and Secretary to Law Department* (1985).

'Documents the subject of secrecy provisions'

For a document to be exempt under this class, the disclosure must constitute 'an offence against an Act'.

Thus, although disobedience to a statute amounts to a common law misdemeanour (see *East Suffolk Rivers Catchment Board v Kent* (1941)), there must still be an offence against an Act (and not merely a simple prohibition against disclosure).

In addition, a document is not exempt unless disclosure to the applicant would constitute such a statutory offence. If disclosure to the applicant can be effected lawfully, the document is not an exempt document under this class.

'Documents containing confidential material'

The following must be considered in deciding whether an obligation of confidence exists:

- whether the information is confidential;
- whether the information was communicated in confidence or in such a way that there was an obligation of confidence;
- whether disclosure would amount to authorised use by the confidant although not necessarily with a prejudicial or detrimental effect: see *Re Maher and the Attorney General's Department and CRA Ltd* (1986).

The exemption extends the protection against disclosure beyond breach of confidence in the accepted understanding of that term as it is known to the law where:

- information is obtained in confidence;
- its disclosure could reasonably be expected to prejudice the future supply of such information to the agency; and
- disclosure would, on balance, be contrary to the 'public interest' (see above).

FOI legislation generally prevents an agency from refusing access to an exempt document if:

- it is practicable to give access to a copy of the document from which the exempt matter has been deleted; and
- it appears to the agency (whether from the terms of the application or after consultation with the applicant) that the applicant would wish to be given access to such a copy.

Reverse FOI

FOI legislation generally contains so called 'reverse FOI' provisions such that where the document is exempt by reason of containing information concerning:

- the *personal affairs* of any person (whether living or dead); or
- the *business, professional, commercial or financial affairs* of any person,

the agency is prevented from giving access to the document (otherwise than to the person concerned):

- unless the agency has taken such steps as are reasonably practicable to obtain the views of the person concerned; and

- if the agency subsequently determines to give access to the document, until after the expiration of the period within which an application for a review or appeal under the relevant legislation may be made or, where such an application is made, until after the application has been finally disposed of: see ss 31 and 32 of the FOI Act 1989 (NSW).

Conclusive certificates

FOI legislation generally contains provision for a claim of exemption in respect of certain classes of 'exempt documents' (for example, cabinet documents) to be made by the issue by a minister of a 'conclusive certificate' that a particular document is exempt.

A claim of exemption is similar to a claim of public interest immunity (see Chapter 7).

Depending upon the wording of the applicable legislation, the 'outside' review or appellate body (see below) may have little or no jurisdiction to investigate a determination where a conclusive certificate has been issued.

Applications to amend records

Once access to a document has been given, FOI legislation generally provides that the applicant may apply to the agency for amendment of the agency's records: see s 39 of the FOI Act 1989 (NSW).

An application to amend records will not be competent unless:

- the document concerns the person's personal affairs; and

- that information is available for use by the agency in connection with its administrative functions; and

- the information is, in the applicant's opinion, incomplete, incorrect, out of date or misleading.

As mentioned above, the expression 'personal affairs' has been held to encompass any matters of private concern to the applicant.

'Incorrect' means not in accordance with fact: see *Re Resch and Department of Veterans' Affairs* (1986).

An agency's record cannot be amended simply because it states correctly what has been determined (for example, the reaching of a medical opinion) such that the claim amounts to a collateral challenge to a decision of the agency: see *Resch*.

However, matters of professional opinion in a record may be challenged where:

- there is no probative material to support the opinion; or
- there has been incompetence, bad faith, bias or inexperience in the person giving the opinion: see *Re Leverett and Australian Telecommunications Commission* (1985).

An agency:

- may refuse to amend its records for any of the reasons set out in the legislation; but
- must inform the applicant of the reasons for refusal and the rights of review and appeal available to the applicant.

The applicant can make a further application requiring the agency to add a notation to the relevant record to the effect that the applicant still claims the record to be incorrect, etc.

The agency must comply with this request and give the applicant written notice of the terms of the notation.

Internal review of determinations of applications

FOI legislation generally makes provision for a right of internal review in relation to both applications for access to documents and applications for amendment of records.

An application for review cannot be dealt with by the person who dealt with the application at first instance, or by a person subordinate to that person: see ss 34(5) and 47(5) of the FOI Act 1989 (NSW).

Ordinarily, the relevant internal review procedures must first be followed before any rights of external review or appeal are exercised.

External review of determinations of applications

FOI legislation generally makes provision for a right of external review by the relevant ombudsman in relation to both applications for access to documents and applications for amendment of records.

The ombudsman is ordinarily precluded from investigating any conduct:

- while the determination is subject to a right of internal review;
- if the determination was subject to such a right but no application for review was made; or
- while any relevant appeal proceedings are before the appellate body.

Appeals with respect to determinations of applications

Any person aggrieved by a determination made by an agency in relation to his or her application for access or amendment of records may appeal to a specified tribunal or court (for example, the relevant Administrative Appeals Tribunal or, in NSW, the Administrative Decisions Tribunal).

Once again, the relevant legislation ordinarily precludes an appeal:

- while the determination is subject to a right of internal review;
- if the determination was subject to such a right but no application for review was made; or
- while any relevant complaint is being investigated by the ombudsman.

12 Privacy Legislation

You should be familiar with the following areas:

- the concept of 'privacy'
- Art 12 of the Universal Declaration of Human Rights
- the objects of the Privacy Act 1988 (Cth)
- the general purposes of Information Privacy Principles ('IPPs') and National Privacy Principles ('NPPs')
- the role of the Privacy Commissioner

Introduction

'Privacy' is a rather elusive cultural construct and can be viewed as a term with referential meaning. Defining 'privacy' is no easy matter, but it is helpful to think in terms of persons having an 'entitlement' to exercise *some* meaningful control over access by others (in particular, governments) to 'personal information', even though such an 'entitlement' will fall short of a legal right to fully determine when, how and to what extent information about them is communicated to others. In the absence of a widely accepted definition of 'privacy', the courts appear reluctant to set strict parameters to protect it.

Australia has ratified various international covenants that recognise the existence of a right of privacy, including the *Universal Declaration of Human Rights*, adopted in 1948. Article 12 provides: 'No one shall be subjected to arbitrary interference with his privacy, family home, or correspondence, nor to attacks upon his honour or reputation. Everyone has the right to protection against such interference or attacks.' The European Convention on Human Rights (1950) re-affirms the Declaration. Finally, the International Covenant on Civil and Political Rights (1966) protects against interference with privacy that is arbitrary, abusive or unlawful.

However, there is in Australia no specific 'right to privacy' as such and, at present, the common law in this country has not developed to a point where a tort of invasion of privacy has been recognised: see *Australian Broadcasting Corporation v Lenah Game Meats Pty Ltd* (2001). Nevertheless, there are in existence throughout Australia a number of statutes, both federal and State, in relation to privacy and the protection of personal information. This chapter is intended only to provide a general overview of the Privacy Act 1988 (Cth) (hereafter the 'Privacy Act').

Objects of the Privacy Act 1988

The Privacy Act was passed by federal Parliament at the end of 1988. The legislation gave effect to Australia's:

- agreement to implement Guidelines adopted in 1980 by the Organisation for Economic Co-operation and Development (OECD) for the Protection of Privacy and Transborder Flows of Personal Data; and
- obligations under Art 17 of the International Covenant on Civil and Political Rights (1966).

Government sector

The Privacy Act, when originally enacted, had two main objectives:

- to protect personal information in the possession of federal government departments and agencies; and
- to introduce and ensure safeguards for the collection and use of tax file numbers (the latter connected with the upgrading of the tax file number system following the demise of the 'Australia Card' proposal).

Eleven Information Privacy Principles ('IPPs'), which are based on the OECD guidelines, set out strict safeguards for any personal information that is handled by federal government and ACT government agencies. Section 16 of the Privacy Act prohibits breach by an 'agency' (defined in s 6(1) of that Act) of the 11 IPPs set out in s 14 of the Privacy Act.

The IPPs principally cover the collection, storage, access, use and disclosure of this information. The ACT government agencies became bound by the Privacy Act through the passing of the Australian Capital Territory Government Service (Consequential Provisions) Act 1994 (Cth).

Private sector

In December 2000, the *Privacy Amendment (Private Sector) Act 2000* (Cth) was passed by federal Parliament and extended coverage of the Privacy Act to most private sector organisations (other than small businesses operators). The new scheme came into effect for most organisations covered by the Privacy Act on 21 December 2001. Whilst 'employee records' are exempt from the legislation, employers must apply the provisions of the legislation to independent contractors and to personal information gathered about an employee, that is, information that is not related to the performance of an employee's duties.

The 10 National Privacy Principles (NPPs) in the Privacy Act regulate how private sector organisations should collect, use, disclose, keep secure and provide access to personal information. Briefly, the NPPs cover matters such as the collection of information, the use and disclosure of information, accessing and correcting information, the use of sensitive information and employer openness in the conduct of privacy policy. The principles give individuals a right to know what information an organisation holds about them and a right to correct that information if it is wrong. The Federal Privacy Commissioner has produced Guidelines to the National Privacy Principles to assist private sector organisations to meet their obligations in the handling of personal information.

The Privacy Commissioner

Section 27 of the Privacy Act sets out the general functions of the Privacy Commissioner, who has the power to investigate an act or practice of an agency or other organisation that may breach an IPP or NPP. Where appropriate, the Privacy Commissioner endeavours to effect a resolution by conciliation. Determinations that compensation be paid for loss suffered as a result of a breach can also be made.

A brief summary of privacy principles

Although the exact nature of the relevant obligations varies somewhat depending upon the applicable set of privacy principles, it is ordinarily the case under privacy legislation that personal information must be collected:

- for lawful purposes directly related to a function or activity of the organisation and where the collection is necessary for that purpose;
- from the individual to whom the information relates, unless otherwise authorised or where the information is collected under an applicable exception;
- in circumstances where the individual from whom it is collected is made aware of the following matters: the fact that it is being collected, the purpose for collecting it, intended recipients of the information, whether the supply is mandatory or voluntary, relevant rights to access and correct the information, and the name and address of the collecting organisation and any holding organisation; and
- taking reasonable steps to ensure the information is relevant, accurate, not excessive and up to date and that the collection does not unreasonably intrude on the individual's personal affairs.

Also, where organisations store personal information they must:

- ensure that it is kept no longer than necessary and disposed of appropriately, is protected by reasonable security safeguards, and is protected from unauthorised use or disclosure when made available to a third party for a provision of a service to the organisation;
- provide individuals with sufficient information about the organisation's holdings of personal information to enable the individual to exercise relevant rights (including rights to have records containing personal information amended in certain circumstances);
- provide individuals with access to personal information about themselves without unreasonable delay and expense; and
- comply with individual requests to amend their personal information to ensure that it is relevant, up to date, complete and not misleading.

Organisations proposing to use or disclose personal information must:

- take reasonable steps to ensure its accuracy before use;
- use it only for the purpose for which it was collected, for a directly related purpose, for a purpose to which the individual has consented, where the use is necessary to prevent or lessen a threat to life or health or subject to an applicable exception;
- only disclose it for a purpose directly related to a purpose of collection and where the individual is unlikely to object, where the individual has been put on notice that information is usually disclosed to the relevant person or body, where the disclosure is necessary to prevent or lessen a threat to life or health, or subject to an applicable exception; and
- not disclose personal information about a person's ethnic or racial origin, political opinions, religious or philosophical beliefs or trade union membership unless disclosure is necessary to prevent or lessen a threat to life or health or is subject to an applicable exception.

Other additions to the Federal Privacy Commissioner's jurisdiction

In 1989, the Federal Privacy Commissioner was given additional functions in relation to 'spent convictions' information. The following year, two major additions were made in the areas of credit reporting and data matching.

The credit reporting jurisdiction (see Part IIIA of the Privacy Act) was the first major extension of the Privacy Act to a private sector area of activity and generated significant involvement with the private sector in the development of legally binding rules for the handling of credit information. For example, personal information is not to be given to certain persons carrying on credit reporting. In addition, certain information is to be given if an individual's application for credit is refused. There are also limits on the use of personal information obtained from credit providers.

The data matching jurisdiction led to the creation of a separate unit within the Privacy Commissioner's office (located in Canberra) dedicated to the oversight of the Commissioner's responsibilities under the Data-matching Program (Assistance and Tax) Act 1990 (Cth).

The Federal Privacy Commissioner acquired additional functions under amendments to the National Health Act 1953 (Cth), passed in

1991 in relation to guidelines for the operation of the eligibility checking system between pharmacists and the Health Insurance Commission.

A new function was conferred on the Federal Privacy Commissioner by the Telecommunications Act 1997 (Cth) in relation to records made by telecommunications carriers, carriage service providers and others of their disclosures of customer information. The Act also provides for industry codes and standards of conduct in a range of consumer protection areas, including privacy. The Privacy Commissioner must be consulted on any privacy codes and standards.

Index